LET'S STUDY EPHESIANS

In the same series:

LET'S STUDY MATTHEW by Mark E. Ross
LET'S STUDY MARK by Sinclair B. Ferguson
LET'S STUDY LUKE by Douglas J. W. Milne
LET'S STUDY JOHN by Mark G. Johnston
LET'S STUDY ACTS by Dennis E. Johnson
LET'S STUDY 1 CORINTHIANS by David Jackman
LET'S STUDY 2 CORINTHIANS by Derek Prime
LET'S STUDY GALATIANS by Derek Thomas
LET'S STUDY PHILIPPIANS by Sinclair B. Ferguson
LET'S STUDY COLOSSIANS & PHILEMON by Mark G. Johnston
LET'S STUDY 1 & 2 THESSALONIANS by Andrew W. Young
LET'S STUDY 1 TIMOTHY by W. John Cook
LET'S STUDY HEBREWS by Hywel R. Jones
LET'S STUDY 1 PETER by William W. Harrell
LET'S STUDY 2 PETER & JUDE by Mark G. Johnston
LET'S STUDY THE LETTERS OF JOHN by Ian Hamilton
LET'S STUDY REVELATION by Derek Thomas

Series Editor: SINCLAIR B. FERGUSON

Let's Study
EPHESIANS

Sinclair B. Ferguson

THE BANNER OF TRUTH TRUST

THE BANNER OF TRUTH TRUST

Head Office
3 Murrayfield Road
Edinburgh, EH12 6EL
UK

North America Office
PO Box 621
Carlisle, PA 17013
USA

banneroftruth.org

First published 2005

Reprinted 2008, 2011, 2015, 2021

*

ISBN: 978 0 85151 907 4

*

Typeset in 11/12.5 Ehrhardt MT
at The Banner of Truth Trust, Edinburgh

Printed in the USA by
Versa Press Inc.,
East Peoria, IL.

For

JOHN AND SUSAN RUSHTON:

Long-Time Friends

One-Time Colleagues

Always Encouragers

Contents

PUBLISHER'S PREFACE ix

INTRODUCTION xi

1. Dear Ephesians (1:1–2) 1
2. A Sentence Begun in Eternity (1:3–6) 7
3. Grace Makes Us Rich (1:7–10) 12
4. Sovereign Blessings (1:11–14) 16
5. Reasons to Pray (1:15–18) 21
6. Hope and Riches (1:15–19) 25
7. The Power-full Church (1:18–23) 30
8. Dead or Alive? (2:1–3) 35
9. Children of Wrath? (2:1–3) 40
10. But God (2:4–7) 45
11. Grace Works (2:8–10) 50
12. Past Division (2:11–12) 54
13. The Big Picture (2:13–16) 59
14. But Now (2:17–18) 65
15. Fellow Citizens (2:19–22) 69
16. Prisoner of Christ, Steward of the Mystery (3:1–6) 74
17. Unsearchable Riches (3:7–9) 79
18. Multi-Coloured Wisdom (3:8–13) 84

19.	Bending the Knee (3:14–19)	89
20.	To God Be the Glory (3:20–21)	94
21.	The One and the Many (4:1–6)	98
22.	Each One Has One (4:7–12)	102
23.	The Goal of Ministry (4:11–16)	109
24.	New Life for Old (4:17–24)	115
25.	Become What You Are (4:25–32)	121
26.	Walking in Love (5:1–8)	127
27.	Walking in the Light (5:8–14)	132
28.	Walking in Wisdom (5:15–17)	137
29.	Filled with the Spirit (5:18–21)	142
30.	Wives and Their Husbands (5:22–24)	147
31.	Husbands and Their Wives (5:25–33)	153
32.	Children and Parents (6:1–4)	157
33.	Parents and Children (6:4)	162
34.	Slaves and Masters (6:5–9)	167
35.	Life Is a Battle (6:10–12)	172
36.	The Armour of God (6:13–17)	178
37.	All Prayer (6:18–20)	184
38.	Final Greetings (6:21–24)	190

GROUP STUDY GUIDE 195

FOR FURTHER READING 207

Publisher's Preface

Let's Study Ephesians is part of a series of books which seek to explain and apply the message of Scripture. The series is designed to meet a specific and important need in the church. While not technical commentaries, the volumes comment on the text of a biblical book; and, without being merely lists of practical applications, they are concerned with the ways in which the teaching of Scripture can affect and transform our lives today. Understanding the Bible's message and applying its teaching are the aims.

Like other volumes in the series, *Let's Study Ephesians* seeks to combine explanation and application. Its concern is to be helpful to ordinary Christian people by encouraging them to understand the message of the Bible and apply it to their own lives. The reader in view is not the person who is interested in all the detailed questions which fascinate the scholar, although behind the writing of each study lies an appreciation for careful and detailed scholarship. The aim is exposition of Scripture written in the language of a friend, seated alongside you with an open Bible.

Let's Study Ephesians is designed to be used in various contexts. It can be used simply as an aid for individual Bible study. Some may find it helpful to use in their devotions with husband or wife, or to read in the context of the whole family.

In order to make these studies more useful, not only for individual use but also for group study in Sunday School classes and home, church or college, study guide material will be found on pp. 195–205. Sometimes we come away frustrated rather than helped by group discussions. Frequently that is because we have been encouraged to discuss a passage of Scripture which we do not understand very well in the first place. Understanding must always be the foundation for enriching discussion and for thoughtful, practical application. Thus, in addition to the exposition of Ephesians, the additional material provides questions to encourage personal thought and study, or to be used as discussion starters. The Group Study Guide divides the material into thirteen sections and provides direction for leading and participating in group study and discussion.

Introduction

Romans is, humanly speaking, the most impressive of Paul's letters. But Ephesians is probably the most elegant. In its opening doxology blessings cascade down upon the reader. In its closing verses the smell of the battlefield lies heavily in the air and through the smoke of war we see Christians, fully clad in the armour of spiritual warfare, still standing. From beginning to end Ephesians sets before us the wonder of God's grace, the privilege of belonging to the church, and the pattern of life-transformation the gospel produces.

How appropriate that this panorama is set before us by a man whose name was Paul (*paulus* in Latin meant 'the little one'). Here the apostle, who considered himself the 'lower-least' of all the saints, expounds for the Ephesians 'the unsearchable riches of Christ' (*Eph*. 3:8). Although born a Jew, and named after Israel's first King, Saul, he does this as 'a prisoner for Christ Jesus on behalf of . . . Gentiles' (*Eph*. 3:1).

How did this remarkable situation come about? Paul gives the fundamental answer in chapter three. But before we reach that point in his letter, it is helpful to ask some questions: What brought about his writing to the Ephesians? Who were they and how did he know them? Where was he when he wrote to them as a 'prisoner'? Why was he writing to them? What was his message?

THE EPHESIANS

Ephesus was the major city of the Roman province known as Asia, in what we now think of as Turkey. An ancient city with a chequered history, it had become part of the Roman Empire two centuries before Paul visited it around AD 52. By ancient standards it was large and heavily populated (a population of perhaps as many as 300,000). Its theatre was the size of a football stadium and may have held as many as 50,000 people.

Here, as a great city of the Roman Empire, the cult of Emperor worship was encouraged. But the religion for which Ephesus was famed was the cult of *Diana* (otherwise known by the Greek name *Artemis*).

Here stood the great Temple of Diana, so magnificent in size and architecture that it ranked as one of the ancient Seven Wonders of the World. It would have dwarfed the Parthenon at Athens. Within the temple was preserved an image of the 'goddess' herself which it was believed had fallen from heaven: 'Who is there that does not know that the city of the Ephesians is temple keeper of the great Artemis, and of the sacred stone that fell from the sky?' was the city's proud boast (*Acts* 19:35).

Paul had come to Ephesus first during his second missionary journey, which had also taken him to Philippi, Thessalonica, Athens, and Corinth. As he customarily did, he preached first to the local Jews (of whom there was a substantial colony). But he did not remain long. *En route* to Ephesus he had been accompanied by Priscilla and Aquila. He left them there to continue the work and moved on. In Paul's absence Apollos arrived, preaching about Jesus, yet apparently without a full knowledge of the gospel. He had known 'only the baptism of John' (*Acts* 18:25). Priscilla and Aquila helped him to a full understanding of Christ. But his earlier deficiencies may explain the existence of a small group in Ephesus whom Paul later encountered who had received only John's baptism (*Acts* 19:3). They, like Apollos, needed further instruction.

Paul later returned to Ephesus (*Acts* 19:1) and remained there for over two years. The record of his ministry is found in Acts 19:1–20:6 and his own reflections on it are described in Acts 20:17–38. These passages should be read in conjunction with his letter, since they help us to understand how Paul's teaching would have been understood by Christians who had seen it worked out in practice.

PAUL

Paul says very little in this letter about his personal circumstances. We know that he was a prisoner when he wrote it (3:1; 4:1; 6:20).

Paul seems to have written four letters from prison around this time: Ephesians, Philippians, Colossians, and Philemon. The last two letters clearly belong together. Tychicus, who served as a kind of apostolic delegate to these churches, was accompanying a runaway slave Onesimus, who had recently come to faith, back to his master Philemon in Colossae. He seems to have been carrying the letter to the Ephesians with him at the same time, and perhaps also a letter Paul calls 'the letter from Laodicaea' (*Col.* 4:16). This letter was to be read to the Colossian congregation and the letter to the Colossians likewise read to the Laodiceans.

We cannot be absolutely certain where Paul was when he wrote. We know that prior to his final imprisonment (during which he wrote again to Ephesus, but this time more personal letters to Timothy), he was imprisoned in other places.

Some have conjectured that he may even have been imprisoned in Ephesus at the time when Aristarchus 'my fellow prisoner' (*Col.* 4:10) was arrested (*Acts* 19:29). This would certainly reduce the distance Onesimus had travelled in his flight from his master Philemon, and also the distance Tychicus would have to travel to see him home and to deliver the letters. But in this case it is unlikely that he would have needed to write a letter to the Ephesians.

Caesarea, where Paul was held for over two years is also a possibility (*Acts* 23:23-26:32). Rome, the traditional setting, remains the most likely place. Certainly Aristarchus who was with him when he wrote Colossians (*Col.* 4:10) seems to have accompanied Paul to Rome and remained with him (*Acts* 27:2).

Imprisonment did not discourage Paul. He had learned to be content wherever he was and whatever his condition (*Phil.* 4:10-13). He knew that the providence of God superintends every detail of his children's lives (see *Phil.* 1:12-18). Ephesians as a whole makes this even clearer. Here Paul, 'the caged bird', sings from a full heart about the grace of God in the gospel. He is a prisoner, yet the gospel has set him inwardly free.

THE LETTER

But why is Paul writing this letter? His comments on the immediate situation are very limited, apart from his promise of and request for prayer (1:16; 3:14; 6:18-20) and his closing greetings. He tells the Ephesians that he has sent Tychicus to 'tell you everything . . . that you may know how we are, and that he may encourage your hearts' (6:21, 22). No doubt he wanted to relieve the Ephesians about how he was responding to his imprisonment. Perhaps he was also anxious to hear how the church was progressing.

There are, however, several unusual features about this letter. First, Ephesians has none of the personal greetings present in the two letters which accompanied this one (*Col.* 4:7–17; *Philem.* 23-24). In addition, Paul appears to believe that not all those who received his letter would have known him personally (3:2). How could this be if he had been their minister for several years?

In addition, in some of the earliest manuscript copies of the Greek New Testament (or of parts of it) the words 'in Ephesus' (1:1) are absent. This has led to the suggestion that perhaps this letter was originally written to more than one congregation. To be more precise, perhaps Tychicus carried several copies of this letter and left a copy with more than one church. This would explain why the letter contains no personal comments ('Tychicus will tell you everything', 6:21). It might also explain the enigmatic reference to a Laodicean letter in Colossians 4:16. Perhaps that letter was a copy of Ephesians. This would explain why Paul tells the Colossians and Laodiceans to exchange the letters they have received from him, but encourages neither to read Ephesians.

We will probably never discover the details of the circumstances in which Ephesians was written. Thinking of it as a circular letter certainly makes sense of both its style and its contents. But whether or not it was so in first century Asia, it is a circular to the whole church of Jesus Christ today! Once we have sought to hear what the Spirit was saying to the Ephesians we need to listen to what he is saying to the churches today through the Letter to the Ephesians.

THE MESSAGE

What was Paul's message? He wanted to encourage his fellow Christians. Perhaps one reason for sending his friend Tychicus was his confidence that, if need be, he would be able to help the Ephesians understand and apply what the letter contained.

Doubtless the Ephesians – like ourselves – needed encouragement. Even if there were several house churches in the city the number of believers must have been dwarfed by the overwhelming numbers of their pagan neighbours. They could still remember the day when some of them had been manhandled and dragged into the city theatre. For two hours up to 50,000 of their fellow-citizens had shouted out at the top of their voices the deafening chant 'Great is Artemis [Diana] of the Ephesians' (*Acts* 19:28–34). The magnificent temple, the antagonism of the craftsmen, the 'Diana tourist industry' – all this, coupled with an interest in the occult in Ephesus, must at times have seemed intimidating to the small group of new believers.

The Ephesian Christians were marginalized in a pluralistic culture tolerant of many things but not of the Christian gospel or the church which proclaimed it.

They needed to know that they were *secure* – Paul teaches them that they are *anchored in the eternal purposes of God.* They lived under the threat of *dark and sinister powers* – they needed to know that Christ had conquered *all his and their enemies.* They were surrounded by the influence of *the world, the flesh, and the devil* –they needed to know that *God had raised them out of that spiritual death.* They were confronted on a daily basis with Gentile *paganism* – they needed to know that Christ had brought them into *the family of God.* They lived under the shadow of *a false temple* and *a false idol* – they needed to know that they were *the true temple of God.* They lived in an *ungodly society* – they needed to know how *the gospel would transform their lives.* They saw life in marriage, family and business *corrupted* by self-interest - they needed to know how grace could *transform* all relationships. They were under *attack* from the forces of darkness – they needed to know how they could *remain standing* in the battle.

This, and much else, Paul unfolds in a letter only four pages long. It will take us the rest of our lives to understand and apply it. Because it is part of God-breathed Scripture, we can turn to it in the confidence that it will teach, rebuke, transform, and equip us (*2 Tim.* 3:16-17). May it have that impact on our lives, as it has had on countless Christians down through the centuries!

I

Dear Ephesians

Paul, an apostle of Christ Jesus by the will of God, to the saints who are in Ephesus, and are faithful in Christ Jesus: [2]Grace to you and peace from God our Father and the Lord Jesus Christ. (Eph. 1:1–2)

Ancient correspondence – like its contemporary counterparts – opened according to a traditional formula. Our practice is to write the recipient's name at the beginning and leave the author's signature to the end. Modern e-mails have reverted to the more sensible ancient form in which the names of both the writer and the recipient were given first, usually followed by some word of greetings.

Paul adopted this basic formula in almost all of his letters. Only in his strongly worded letter to the Galatians did he refrain from all expressions of thankfulness to God for his blessings on the recipients. He did not despise the good natural customs of his society.

But while Paul employs cultural traditions, he always bends them back into the gospel and thus transforms them. He takes what is natural, and into it he pours God's grace. Thus here formal greetings are replaced by a fine expression of Christian love set within the context of the saving work of God.

Paul identifies himself as the author, describes his readers, and sends his greetings.

THE AUTHOR: PAUL

The opening words reveal both the name (*Paul*) and the status (*apostle*) of the author.

The Acts of the Apostles marks a transition in the name by which this unlikely apostle was known – a change from Saul to Paul. The turning point is recorded in Acts 13:9 ('But Saul, who was also called Paul . . .'). Although the name 'Saul' appears on three more occasions in Acts, these are all flashbacks to his calling on the Damascus Road and its aftermath (*Acts* 22:7, 13; 26:14).

This change of name took place at the beginning of the Antioch Church's outreach mission. Possibly Saul's name was changed then to a less obviously Jewish one, for the sake of his leadership of the mission to the Gentiles (*Gal.* 1:16; 2:7–8).

It is equally possible however that from childhood Saul had two 'given' names. His home town, Tarsus, was a cosmopolitan city. It had, for those days, a huge population – probably greater than that of Scotland in the first century!

Since the time of Pompey (106–48 BC) citizens of Tarsus had enjoyed the privilege of Roman citizenship. Paul used this to advantage on more than one occasion (*Acts* 16:37; 21:37–40; 22:24–29). Thus by birth he was a citizen of two worlds, a Hebrew of Hebrews (*Phil.* 3:5), but also a citizen of Rome. He was Saul, proud descendant of Benjamin. But he was also Paul, free-born Roman citizen.

The context in which the name change takes place suggests that even if Saul had received two 'given' names in childhood, 'Paul' now came to the fore in order that he might become 'all things to all people, that by all means I might save some. I do it all for the sake of the gospel . . . ' (*1 Cor.* 9:22–23).

It is worth remembering who and what Paul was. He was an amazingly influential Christian, but he was often persecuted in the world and demeaned and despised within the church. In his own eyes he was 'the very least of all the saints' (3:8). Ancient literature provides us with only one physical description of Paul. It is found in the apocryphal *Acts of Paul and Thecla* (originally composed probably in the second century): He was 'a man little of stature, thin haired upon the head, crooked in the legs, of good state of body, with eyebrows joining, and nose somewhat hooked.'

Given Paul's status in the Christian church, perhaps the unimpressive nature of the description suggests some degree of authenticity. For all that, however, there was another aspect to him which the same document mentions: 'Sometimes he appeared like a man, and sometimes he had the face of an angel.' The language obviously echoes the description of the martyr Stephen (*Acts* 6:15), but in so doing gives an indication of how venerated Paul's ministry continued to be. He was a small man who became great.

It was *by the will of God* that Paul was *an apostle of Christ Jesus*. The Greek word *apostolos* means 'a sent one'. It was sometimes used in classical literature for a naval expedition, the commander of which might also be known as an *apostolos*. The authority of an apostle to speak and act was therefore dependent on the nature of the authority of his sender. That is why it is important to notice that the word is used in more than one way in the New Testament.

- It is used of Jesus himself (*Heb.* 3:1) as the Son whom God sent into the world (*John* 3:17).
- It is used of 'the twelve' whom Jesus called and trained to be part of the foundation of the church (cf. *Eph.* 2:20).
- It is sometimes used of believers commissioned by their congregation for special service. In this sense, 'apostle' and 'missionary' mean basically the same. The former term is derived from the Greek, the latter from the Latin, verbs 'to send'. Barnabas and Saul were both apostles in this sense (*Acts* 14:14) – sent out by the church at Antioch.

But Paul was conscious that he was also, and more fundamentally, an apostle not only of Antioch but *of Christ Jesus*. He had received a direct commission from the Lord Jesus himself, just as really as had Peter or James or John. He was emphatic about this, especially when his calling was demeaned and under attack, as it was in the churches in Corinth and Galatia (see *1 Cor.* 9:1; 15:3–10; *2 Cor.* 11–12; *Gal.* 1:11ff.). This explains why his letters carry such a weighty sense of his own authority.

Central to the apostles' ministry was a calling to be the vehicle of God's revelation. Jesus had made this clear in the upper room, shortly before his death (*John* 14:24–5; 16:12–15; 17:18). He had breathed his Spirit on them in order to equip them for this ministry (*John* 20:22). They did foundation work (*Eph.* 3:4–5). And although Paul felt himself 'born' into this office in a different way ('one untimely born' as he describes himself in *1 Cor.* 15:8), he claimed to have the mind of Christ and the gift of the Spirit for this ministry (*1 Cor.* 2:6–13). It was Christ's authority ultimately, not Paul's, that he expressed. It was therefore Christ's authority to reign and rule in the churches that was at stake.

In Ephesians, Paul gives us a number of hints as to what this calling involved. With authority came responsibility. He was called to expound the gospel (3:7–8), to be a man of intercessory prayer caring for the church (1:15ff., 3:14ff.), and to be willing to suffer for Christ and his people. In fact he wrote this letter while he was a prisoner (3:1; 4:1). At every level of Christian service these are always the things that equip us to serve Christ well.

Thus Paul – the littlest one – was enabled to fulfil his calling. He had a deep consciousness that it was God, not man, nor even his own aspirations that had brought him into the service of the Lord Jesus Christ.

THE RECIPIENTS: THE EPHESIANS

The readers of this letter are described in several ways. They are *saints*, they are *at Ephesus*, and they are also *faithful in Christ Jesus*.

According to the New Testament all Christians – young and old, rich and poor, wise and simple – are *saints*. They have been set apart ('sanctified') or reserved for God's special purposes. For Paul, becoming holy is the natural fruit of becoming a saint. For a person becomes a saint not by years of hard effort leading to promotion among the spiritual élite when the Christian life ends, but by the spiritual resurrection and transformation with which it begins.

These saints are also *faithful*. Faithfulness describes their response to God's grace – they were full of trust that led to obedience.

The combination of these two terms summarises the structure of this whole letter. In the first half (1:3–3:21), Paul describes the work of God in setting apart the Ephesians as saints. In the second half (4:1–6:20), he summons them to live as those whose lives are set apart for God.

LEARNING GOSPEL GRAMMAR

We cannot understand or use a language without knowing the basic rules of its grammar. The same is true of the gospel. It has a grammar.

That grammar is very clearly illustrated in Paul's letter to the Ephesians.

The first part of the letter contains statements in which the verbs are almost exclusively in what is called the indicative mood: they tell us what God has already done for us in Christ. In fact only once in the first three chapters does Paul urge us to do anything – and that is to 'remember' what we once were but no longer are (2:11)! By contrast, the second part of the letter is full of imperatives! Dozens of them!

Understanding what the gospel is and how it works hinges on grasping the relationship between the indicative and imperative moods in Paul's teaching. Everything he urges us to do (4:1ff.) is dependent on everything he tells us God has already done (1:2ff.). Our faithfulness is a response to God's grace.

We also need to have a firm grasp of a second pair of ideas, which Paul expresses right at the start of the letter. These *saints* seem to be in two places at once! They are *in Christ* but they are also *at Ephesus*. These two locations frame the whole of Paul's message. In chapters 1–3 he is describing what it means to be *in Christ* – how that has been planned and accomplished. In chapters 4–6 he is describing how to work out this new life while still living *at Ephesus*. The rest of the letter works through both of these aspects in great detail. It is therefore important for us, first of all, to appreciate the inbuilt and underlying structure and logic of Ephesians – for it is the structure and logic of the gospel.

APOSTOLIC GREETINGS

Ancient letters opened with greetings. Paul transforms the usual formula, elevating it to new heights. As an apostle, he writes with Christ's authority. He wishes them nothing less than *grace and peace* – from both the Father and his Son.

Grace is God's amazing favour and love, not only unmerited by us but also actually de-merited. This letter is full of it (see 1:6, 7; 2:4–5; 3:2, 8). This single word summarises the first three chapters Paul is about to write, in which he will expound its origin and the means by which he expresses it.

Peace is the Old Testament's '*shalom*' – not just a feeling of quiet, but the well-being of our whole lives. It is what Paul goes on to describe in the second half of Ephesians: reconciliation in Christ which creates unity-in-diversity in the new community of the church (4:1–16), transformation in the way we live (4:17–5:21), and strength to remain standing in the spiritual battle (6:10–20).

Interestingly, Paul's conclusion (6:23–4) reverses the order of his introduction. There he wishes peace (6:23) and grace (6:24). Is this a hint that, between the two bookends of his letter, grace will lead to peace, and peace will always rest in grace? How marvellous!

Where do you live? Not *at Ephesus*. But perhaps London, or Sydney, or Washington D.C.? In Africa or Asia, Latin America or Australasia? But do you share a more fundamental sphere of residence, a deeper ethnicity? Are your real roots *in Christ*?

If so, those around you may be thinking what people in Ephesus were probably thinking about these young Christians: 'They seem to belong somewhere else.'

We do. No matter where Christians live, they ultimately belong *in Christ*. What this means Paul explains in the course of the six chapters that follow. We need to read on!

2

A Sentence Begun in Eternity

Blessed be the God and Father of our Lord Jesus Christ, who has blessed us in Christ with every spiritual blessing in the heavenly places, [4]*even as he chose us in him before the foundation of the world, that we should be holy and blameless before him. In love* [5]*he predestined us for adoption through Jesus Christ, according to the purpose of his will,* [6]*to the praise of his glorious grace, with which he has blessed us in the Beloved.* (Eph. 1:3–6)

Paul is already teaching us to use the 'grammar' of the gospel. It is because we receive grace that we become faithful; because we are 'in Christ' we can be 'saints' even if we live in Ephesus.

What follows, however, almost suggests that Paul cared very little about ordinary grammar! While verses 3–14 are broken down into five sentences in our translation, they are actually only one sentence in Greek – stretching to over two hundred words! They constitute a doxology, a poem of praise to God for all the blessings of the gospel.

God is to be *blessed* because he has *blessed* us (verse 3). 'Bless' here means 'to speak well' of someone. We speak well of the Lord (*Blessed be . . . God*) because in Christ, the Living Word, he has spoken well of (*blessed*) us.

EVERY SPIRITUAL BLESSING

Receiving grace leads to enjoying *every spiritual blessing* – many of which Paul mentions in the verses that follow.

The sphere in which these are enjoyed is *the heavenly places* (verse 3). This phrase recurs several times in Ephesians (1:20;

2:6; 3:10; 6:12). It refers to the new realm of spiritual realities into which believers have been brought in Christ. The gospel does not promise material blessings as its central benefit (although its power in a person's life may create greater diligence and wisdom that will lead to such prosperity). In fact the blessings of the gospel are for those who take up the cross and die daily (*Luke* 9:23): suffering with Christ is part of our inheritance in Christ (*Rom.*8:17).

Christ himself is the *source* of these blessings. It is *in Christ* that God blesses us, not apart from him. This expression and its equivalents occur over and over again in these verses ('in Christ', 'through Jesus Christ', 'in him', 'in Christ'). It is Paul's description of a Christian (a word he himself never uses).

The New Testament has a unique way of describing the faith that unites us to Christ. It speaks about believing 'into' Christ.

When we become Christians we do not merely receive a 'benefits package' from Christ – containing forgiveness, new life, new hope and so on. Much more than that is involved: we receive Christ himself. We are united to him by his Spirit so that all that he achieved for us becomes ours. In this sense, says Paul, we died with Christ, were buried and raised with him, ascended with him, reign with him and will be with him when he comes in glory (cf. *Col.* 3:1ff). Here we are given a survey of the superabundance of blessing that comes to us in and with Christ: election, adoption, redemption, sanctification, forgiveness. Big words – big blessings!

Paul even goes so far as to say – *every spiritual blessing* is ours in Christ (verse 3). They are all ours immediately we are *in Christ.*

Why, then, would you look for God's blessing anywhere else than *in Christ*?

BEFORE THE DAWN OF TIME

How have God's blessings in Christ come to us? By faith, as Paul says later (verse 13). But while it is through faith that we are saved (2:8), that faith cannot be our own doing, because by nature we were 'dead' in our sins, captive to the evil one. The spiritually dead are incapable of signs of life. New life must therefore be the result of something God does. The origin of our faith is found in God's action, God's purpose, God's will.

Paul begins with God's purposes and plan. Right at the start he underlines that all the blessings of salvation come to us because he *chose us in him [Christ] before the foundation of the world* (verse 4).

God's grace is *so* gracious that he had us in view before we came to faith, even before we were born, even before the world was created! Then – when only Father, Son and Holy Spirit existed (notice how he mentions all three persons of the Godhead in this section) – in the love which these persons have for each other, and for all they are as God – God lovingly predestined his people to be his (verse 4–5).

This is God's eternal election.

If we ask 'Why did he choose me?' the only answer is: 'He loved you.' If we then ask: 'Yes, but why did he love me?' the only answer is 'Because he loved you and planned to bring glory to his grace in and through you'.

But surely there must be some other reason? What was there about me that made him love me? Did he see that I was the kind of person who would trust him? No! How muddle-headed such an idea is! I am 'the kind of person' who is dead in sins, without hope, at enmity with God. There is nothing in me that 'makes' God love me. The reason for his love lies in himself! It is grace from start to finish; nothing but sheer grace.

When we see this we begin to understand why so much talk about 'free will' is muddle-headed. My will is certainly 'free' but only in the sense that it is not coerced. It is never free from who I am, as if I could will 'out of character'. No, what passes as 'out of character' is not a deviation from what we are but a revelation of it! Thus, because my mind is by nature at enmity with God, inevitably my will opposes him (and opposes his free will! cf. *Rom.* 8:7–8!). I need to be set free from that bondage if I am ever going to want Christ.

It is also muddle-headed to question God's sovereign election of his people by protesting that this is not 'just'. Demand justice (as Portia in Shakespeare's *The Merchant of Venice* saw so clearly) and I am lost and damned:

> *Though justice be thy plea, consider this*
> *That, in the course of justice, none of us*
> *Should see salvation: we do pray for mercy.*[1]

[1] William Shakespeare, *The Merchant of Venice*, Act IV, Scene I.

God would have displayed perfect justice by condemning us all. It is his mercy that is expressed in lovingly choosing to save any of us, even one of us.

Paul's teaching on God's election often provokes controversy. It is also frequently misunderstood – 'If you believe in election there is no point to evangelism', as it is often put. But notice that Paul is teaching election to the very people he himself had evangelised! Election and evangelism are not opposites far less enemies, but friends.

Paul had learned this from his Old Testament. But he has also observed it from personal experience (his own 'free will' led him to seek to destroy the church). Only the intervention of God, rooted in the loving will of God, could save him. That intervention was not an accident. It was planned from the foundation of the world! And what was true of him was, he believed, true of all believers.

The last thing to die in us seems to be the lingering element of pride that says 'there must be some reason *in me* to explain why God loves me.' But as soon as we have thought that way (and how hard it is for us proud sinners *not* to think that way!), we have compromised grace. And compromised grace is grace no longer.

How wonderful, on the other hand, to reflect on the fact that God loved me before I loved him, before I trusted in his Son, even before his Son came, even before the creation of the world. Can his love for me be that big, that long, that deep? Yes, indeed – and if it is rooted in eternity, it will also last for eternity. God always puts the finishing touches to the work he has begun (*Phil.* 1:6).

DESTINATION: HOLINESS

In sports where contact with a ball is involved, a cardinal error is often repeated: taking your eye off the ball. It is easily done. We want to see where we have hit it even before we make contact with it!

We can make a similar mistake with election – we rush to our own conclusions before seeing how the Scriptures unfold the truth and its implications. It is thus often said that if we believed in eternal election we would live any way we wanted – because we would still be 'saved'. But to think that way means that we have taken our eye off the text. We have seen the words 'he chose . . . before the foundation of the world' without reading on to the result . . . *'that we should be holy and blameless before him*' (1:4). We are certainly not chosen because we are holy; but we are chosen in order to become holy!

This is the logic of love – love that has chosen to love us, sacrificed and waited for us, been patient with us – this passionate love of God, once received, does not, indeed cannot, leave us unchanged.

There is a further dimension to this. Paul moves, as it were, from one end of eternity to the other. God set his electing love on us before the world's creation; *he predestined us for adoption* (verse 5). Here and now we have the privilege of calling God '*Abba*, Father'. In the future he will display in us the glory of the full family likeness (cf. *Rom.* 8:15–25, 29). God's glory, God's grace in election, our salvation, holiness of lifestyle, expressing the family likeness – these are not at odds with one another. They belong together.

What difference does this make? It produces humility, the effect of being loved by Eternal Love. It gives us a new sense of dignity, the effect of knowing God himself has loved us. It anchors us in a deep security – God's grip of me goes back into eternity. It makes us want to sing the doxology: *Blessed be the God and Father of our Lord Jesus Christ!*

3

Grace Makes Us Rich

In him we have redemption through his blood, the forgiveness of our trespasses, according to the riches of his grace, [8]*which he lavished upon us, in all wisdom and insight* [9]*making known to us the mystery of his will, according to his purpose, which he set forth in Christ* [10]*as a plan for the fullness of time, to unite all things in him, things in heaven and things on earth.* (Eph. 1:7–10)

Ephesians 1 contains one of the most amazing sentences ever penned in any language. It is like a waterfall pouring from the lips of Paul as he tries to express the wonderful privileges of being a Christian. Its great theme is God's grace. The riches of this grace have been lavished on us in Christ. They lead us, at last, to live 'for the praise of his glory' (verses 12, 14).

But here Paul takes us to the epicentre of God's plan and sets everything else he says in its ultimate context. God has lavished his grace on us *in all wisdom and insight* (verse 8). Why should that be needed? The answer is breathtaking: in Jesus Christ God has made known *the mystery of his will, according to his purpose . . . as a plan for the fullness of time*.

THE GREAT MYSTERY

A *mystery* in biblical language is not a puzzle that is still waiting to be solved, but a secret that can be known only when God reveals it. The Old Testament Scriptures trace the early days of God's single-minded purpose. It was hidden in his heart and mind, but he gave intimations of it in different ways.

The revelation of the Old Testament functioned like scaffolding. It was temporary. But it took its shape from what God had planned in eternity and was building behind the scaffolding of Old Testament history – the coming of Christ. When Christ came the scaffolding had fulfilled its purpose. It has now been dismantled. Now the *mystery* behind the scaffolding stands revealed. We now understand why the scaffolding was shaped as it was. It was Christ-shaped. His coming has been God's purpose all along.

Paul loved to think in this way about God's hidden plan. He uses the term *mystery* seven times in this one letter (1:9; 3:3, 4, 6, 9; 5:32; 6:19). At first sight it might seem that he has several mysteries in view. But always at the back of his mind is the one great mystery revealed in Christ – illustrated in a variety of different ways.

The heart of this mystery is that God plans *to unite all things in him, things in heaven and things on earth* (1:10).

The verb translated *to unite*, means 'to sum up'. Paul uses it in Romans 13:9 when he says that the commandments are 'summed up' by 'love your neighbour as yourself'; keep this command and one will keep them all. The last six commandments are all practical applications of one driving principle: love for the God who has redeemed us and for the neighbour who is beside us.

THE FALL

Because of the Fall the world of men and things has been fractured and fragmented. Disintegration is pervasive. Alienation reigns. Adam's sin plunged into disorder and confusion the whole creation over which he was appointed as God's steward-king. The fallen world no longer 'adds up' to the perfect, harmonious cosmos God brought into being and planned to glorify. Now, in Christ, God means to save his creation, to restore it and to transform it into the glory of its original destiny. This is what Christ came to accomplish.

This is why Paul has so much to say about Jesus as the 'second man' and 'the last Adam' (*1 Cor.* 15:45–49; *Rom.* 5:12–21). By one man, Adam, sin entered the world and death followed in its wake. Only by the work of a second man, another Adam, undoing what the first did, and then accomplishing the very things he failed to do, can the cosmos be reintegrated. Paul's breathtaking vision is that God does this in Jesus Christ.

As we shall see in Ephesians, however, there are three major obstacles to this:

- The rebellion of the dark spiritual powers that lie behind the present disintegration must be suppressed.
- The spiritual death, which has come upon all because of Adam's sin, must be reversed by spiritual resurrection.
- The alienation produced in humanity because of our sin needs to give way to a new reconciliation.

All this is accomplished through *the redemption* that we have in Christ.

REDEMPTION

Paul uses a wide variety of terms to describe the nature of what Christ has done for us. *Redemption* is one of them. Here the background lies in the idea of the deliverance from the bondage of slavery which God had accomplished for his people in the Exodus (*Exod.* 6:6). In that event was hidden the 'mystery' of Christ. He would lead his people out of bondage in a new exodus. On the Mount of Transfiguration he talked with Moses and Elijah about the 'departure (literally: *exodus*) which he was about to accomplish at Jerusalem' (*Luke* 9:31). He would be the true Passover Lamb sacrificed for us (*1 Cor.* 5:7).

This time, however, the bondage was not to Pharaoh, but to Satan, to sin, and to death. By his death on the cross, Christ has justly purchased us back for God at the cost of his own blood (1:7). He has dealt with our guilt, to bring us pardon; he has overcome the cosmic forces of darkness which bound us, he has died to the reign of sin that mastered us, and risen in triumph over all his and our enemies (*Rom.* 6:10). Now, by his Spirit, he leads us into the promised land of freedom in life, fellowship with God, and communion with his people.

Does this mean, then, that Christ has persuaded his Father to do something for us, contrary to the Father's will, or perhaps his better judgment? Are we to envisage the Son persuading the Father to 'give us a break'? No! Paul is speaking all along about *the plan of the Father*! *He* has blessed us; *he* has chosen us; in love *he* predestined us to be adopted sons; *he* has redeemed us; *he* has made known the mystery to us. This, says Paul, amounts to *the riches of his grace, which he lavished upon us* (verses 7, 8).

There is more. God gives his lavish love to us *in all wisdom and insight making known . . . the mystery of his will.* Not only has God demonstrated his love and persuaded us of its wonder and power. He has revealed his ultimate *plan for the fullness of time, to unite all things in him, things in heaven and things on earth* (verse 10). It is conceivable that a poorly-taught Christian might live the whole of life without an awareness of what Paul is teaching here. But surely all suspicion of niggardliness on the part of God dissolves in this sea of generosity. Along with lavish grace comes *wisdom and insight.* God lets us into his secret! As a Father he shares with his children what his long-term plan is!

We need to pause to meditate on the grace Paul is describing here. If we grasp the nature of the love God has demonstrated on the cross (*Rom.* 5:8) we will realize that it is not a reluctant but a lavish love!

How suspicious of God many Christians seem to be. We do not trust him; we doubt his goodness; we taste little of the sweetness of his grace. Here is what will dissolve paralysing fears, cringing doubt, suspicious unbelief: *the riches of his grace . . . lavished upon us* (verses 7–8). And *we have* these riches already in Christ!

Do you live in a growing sense of the superabundant love of God? No wonder Paul later describes God as 'rich in mercy' (2:4)!

Yes, grace makes us rich.

4

Sovereign Blessings

In him we have obtained an inheritance, having been predestined according to the purpose of him who works all things according to the counsel of his will, [12]*so that we who were the first to hope in Christ might be to the praise of his glory.* [13]*In him you also, when you heard the word of truth, the gospel of your salvation, and believed in him, were sealed with the promised Holy Spirit,* [14]*who is the guarantee of our inheritance until we acquire possession of it, to the praise of his glory.* (Eph. 1: 11–14)

God plans to bring this fallen world, governed by apparently random and sometimes chaotic events and disruptions in nature and human life, into a unified cosmos over which Jesus Christ will be King. In fact Christ's reign has already begun. He has already ushered in the kingdom of God.

For the moment that kingdom seems small and undistinguished – like a mustard seed (*Mark.* 4:31). But it will expand to fill the whole earth. The day will come, Paul believes, when every knee will bow before Christ and every tongue confess that he is Lord (cf. *Phil.* 2:10–11). On that day 'the wolf shall dwell with the lamb, and the leopard shall lie down with the young goat, and the calf and the lion and the fattened calf together, and a little child shall lead them . . . the weaned child shall put his hand on the adder's den . . . for the earth shall be full of the knowledge of the Lord as the waters cover the sea' (*Isa.* 11:6–9).

There are obstacles in the way of this grand design. Paul intends to show how, in Christ, God has dealt with them. But in the meantime this is the prospect set before every Christian.

Since we have been adopted into the family of God (verse 5), and become the younger brothers of the heir of all things Jesus Christ (*Heb*. 1:2), all things are ours in him (cf. *1 Cor*. 3:21–2). This is our *inheritance* (verse 11).

Does this seem too much to take in and too good to be true? How can it possibly be that the meek shall inherit the earth (*Matt*. 5:5)? Are we not more likely to lose everything by following Christ?

This deep-seated fear may have burdened these young Christians. They were, after all, in Ephesus. It was a city in which darkness stalked the streets. Granted its powers were depleted since 'a number' of former practitioners of the dark arts had publicly burned somewhere in the region of five million pounds (nine million dollars) worth of books as a sign of their conversion to the Lordship of Christ (*Acts* 19:19). But others remained hardened to the gospel. There were reasons that might have led some to fear that they would not be able to stand in the evil day (6:13).

Paul himself had also warned the elders of the church that 'fierce wolves will come in among you, not sparing the flock; and from among your own selves will arise men speaking twisted things, to draw away the disciples after them' (*Acts* 20:29–30). How then could they feel secure?

The apostle's answer is that just as salvation is to be found in Christ, so there is security in him. For we have been predestined by the will of him *who works all things according to the counsel of his will* (1:11).

There is an ultimate invincibility about the work of God. As Peter puts it, God keeps our final inheritance secure for us – and he keeps us for the inheritance (cf. *1 Pet*. 1:3–5).

THE MEDICINE OF DIVINE SOVEREIGNTY

Ephesians 1:11 may be the strongest and most comprehensive statement about God's absolute sovereignty in the whole of the Bible. He is the One who *works all things according to the counsel of his will*. This is not a user-friendly universe for all and sundry. But Paul is stressing that, whatever the native tendencies of people and things, God works with and through all that happens. The events of history and even of our individual lives are never outside his will and purpose. There are no exceptions.

This is strong medicine for us to swallow. Some Christians find the first taste of it seems bitter. For swallowing it also means swallowing the pride that says: 'I am the master of my fate; I am the captain of my soul' (W. E. Henley). But once pride is dissolved by the absolute Lordship and sovereignty of One who can be trusted absolutely, the effects are wonderfully therapeutic. We begin to recover from the sin-sickness that gripped Adam and Eve in the Garden of Eden; at last we allow God to be God; and we discover that his sovereign purposes – even in the experiences that cause us pain – are for our good (*Rom.* 8:28).

In some ways what Paul goes on to say is a yet more remarkable and liberating discovery: God does all this *to the praise of his glory* (1:12, 14). But his glory is not the enemy of our good. In fact he pursues his own glory in such a way that he simultaneously brings his people most blessing! His pleasure and our blessing are marriage partners! That is a commitment from which he will never withdraw.

JEW FIRST, BUT ALSO GENTILE

Throughout this magnificent single sentence paragraph Paul has been speaking of Christians in the first person plural (*us* or *we* occurs in every verse from verse 3 to verse 12 except verse 10). Here, however, he qualifies the *we* as those *who were the first to hope in Christ* (verse 12). In contrast, in verse 13 he speaks about *you also* . . . What does he mean by this order: *we . . . first . . . you*?

Paul might be speaking from a purely chronological point of view: he was a believer before the Ephesians. But as the letter progresses he continues to distinguish between 'you' and 'us'. The distinction in view is an ethnic one between Jews (of whom Paul was one) and Gentiles (which the Ephesians were, cf. 2:11). In the very context of mentioning this distinction Paul is also indicating that it has been overcome in Christ, since the Ephesians too have '*heard . . . the gospel of your salvation, and believed in him* [Christ]' (1:13). In Christ, Jewish believers and Gentile believers share the same privileges!

INHERITANCE

This sheds light on Paul's use of the word *inheritance*. He is not simply saying that as Christians we enjoy great blessing – an inheritance. He wants us to see that the privileges Gentile Christians receive are the fulfilment of all the covenant blessings God had promised throughout the Old Testament. His ancient people had been promised a land flowing with good things. The covenant with Abraham had promised that the nations of the earth would be blessed through his seed (ESV 'offspring') (*Gen.* 12:1ff.). Now Christ, the Seed, had come (*Gal.* 3:16) and the promises of God had found a resounding 'yes' in him (*2 Cor.* 1:20). The blessings promised to Abraham were being poured out through the Spirit on all nations (*Gal.* 3:13–14). The circumcised Jew who believes in Christ (such as Saul of Tarsus) and the uncircumcised Gentile who believes in Christ, inherit the same fulfilled promises.

Thus, early on in his letter, Paul hints that what he later calls 'the dividing wall of hostility' (2:14) has been broken down in Christ. A major obstacle to God's plan has been overcome. Jew and Gentile who believe kneel before the same Lord and Saviour and receive the identical blessings of grace from his hand.

A SEAL AND A PLEDGE

All of the spiritual blessings we enjoy in Christ are rooted in our election (1:4). That divine decision made about us is confirmed by God's action in us in time. The Ephesians who *heard the word of truth, the gospel of your salvation, and believed in him, were sealed with the promised Holy Spirit, who is the guarantee of our inheritance until we acquire possession of it* (1:13–14).

The most natural reading of Paul's words here is that the hearing, believing, and sealing of the Ephesians belonged together as aspects of the one saving reality. But what does it mean to be *sealed with the promised Holy Spirit*?

In the ancient world a seal provided security and also (because of the unique impression it made on the object it sealed) a confirmation of authenticity and ownership. To be *sealed with the . . Spirit* well expresses Paul's emphasis: there is both the security of forgiveness and assurance of belonging to God given to us in Christ and realized in us by his gift of the Holy Spirit. Paul returns to this theme later when he urges the Ephesians not to 'grieve the Holy Spirit of God, by whom you were sealed for the day of redemption' (4:30).

But is this sealing something the Holy Spirit does, or is it the Holy Spirit himself who is the seal?

Paul seems to be thinking about the Spirit himself being God's seal, since he goes on to say that the Spirit himself is also *the guarantee*, the pledge or 'down payment' of the inheritance we have in Christ (verse 14). His presence in our life is itself God's assurance that every spiritual blessing will be ours. More than that, this 'down payment' is a first instalment of the final consummation of the blessings we will experience in the resurrection.

BLESSED TRINITY

All of this, Paul concludes, is *to the praise of his glory* (1:14). It is the third time a similar refrain has appeared (cf. verses 6, 12).

Notice how this threefold refrain wonderfully underlines the trinitarian nature of the blessings Paul has been describing. They all have their *origin* in the plan of the Father (verse 3: 'blessed be the God and *Father* . . . who has blessed us . . . '). Their accomplishment comes from the work of the Son (verse 7: 'in *him* we have redemption . . . '). Their *application* is effected by the work of the Spirit (verse 13: 'you . . . were sealed with the promised *Holy Spirit*'). The activity of all three persons of the Trinity is needed in order to redeem us!

The salvation in which Paul glories is itself a revelation of God's glory as Father, Son and Holy Spirit. It has taken the energies of the whole Godhead to bring to us the blessings of grace! Each divine person is equally necessary to our enjoyment of these blessings; each person is united in purpose and will with the other persons in order that we might be redeemed.

When we remember – as Paul himself did and would soon urge the Ephesians to do – what we were by nature, 'dead in trespasses and sins . . . ' (2:1), it is not surprising that he now breaks into poetry and song.

The surprising thing would be if he – or we – did not!

5

Reasons to Pray

For this reason, because I have heard of your faith in the Lord Jesus and your love towards all the saints, [16]*I do not cease to give thanks for you, remembering you in my prayers,* [17]*that the God of our Lord Jesus Christ, the Father of glory, may give you a spirit of wisdom and of revelation in the knowledge of him,* [18]*having the eyes of your hearts enlightened, that you may know what is the hope to which he has called you . . .* (Eph. 1: 15–18)

Paul has been singing the praises of the God of all grace. The Christian's life is anchored in Jesus Christ. From our election in him before time began, to the final salvation of which the indwelling Spirit is the guarantee, everything we need to live 'to the praise of his glory' (verse 12, 14) is found in Christ. His grace makes us rich with the blessings of redemption, forgiveness, adoption, and spiritual illumination. These are, in Paul's beautiful expression, 'the riches of his grace, which he lavished upon us' (1:7–8).

The resulting fruit in our lives is manifold: *humility* in the face of God's eternal election; *sanctity* in our lifestyle because he has chosen us to be holy; *stability* because we know that we are anchored into the eternal heart of God; *doxology* because we have been so richly and fully blessed.

When Saul of Tarsus first experienced this grace it turned him into a man of prayer (cf. *Acts* 9:11). Even now, perhaps two decades or so later, we find him still on his knees (cf. 3:14). The adoration of the Lord in his grace always led him to intercession for his brothers and sisters.

INFORMATION PROMPTS INTERCESSION

Paul prays with thanksgiving for the Ephesians (and, presumably others in the same region who received his letter). He has *heard* of their transformed lives. Two hallmarks dominated the report he received about them: their *faith in the Lord Jesus* and their *love towards all the saints* (1:15). These constitute the two features Paul always seemed to look for as marks of genuine conversion (as his frequent reference to them in other passages indicates: cf. *1 Cor.* 13:13; *Gal.* 5:6; *Eph.* 6:23; *1 Thess.* 1:3; 3:6; *1 Tim.* 1:14; *2 Tim.* 1:13; 3:10; *Titus.* 2:2; *Philem.* 5). Authentic Christianity always transforms both the Godward and the manward dimensions of life. Otherwise our professions of faith are hollow.

But, in addition to this, it is also clear that Paul's prayer life was fuelled by news about his fellow Christians. A glance at the number of names mentioned in his other letters indicates how much he seemed to know even about churches he had not personally visited. The closing greetings of his letter to the Romans are a remarkable illustration of this. Paul well illustrated the lifestyle he longed to see in others: he prayed for them because he shared their *love towards all the saints* (verse 15).

In passing here we might note that Paul's knowledge of his readers' spiritual growth, but the absence of personal greetings, tends to confirm that this was indeed a 'circular' letter and not one written specifically to Ephesus.

What about our church life, if prayer is the true evidence of love? This challenge is made even more penetrating as Paul adds another feature that marked his prayer life: his thankfulness: *I do not cease to give thanks for you* (verse 16). This is the speech of a man who is marked by God's grace. Gratitude is always the result.

Man is by nature ungrateful (cf. *Rom.* 1:21). We live in ungrateful times (*2 Tim.* 3:2). Many Christians' lives have been marred by this spirit of the age. We fail to give thanks because we do not lift our eyes to the throne from which all blessings flow. Such ingratitude, Paul teaches us by implication, cannot breathe in an atmosphere of true prayer.

KNOWING GOD

For what, then, does Paul pray? First, that the Ephesians will be given *a spirit of wisdom and of revelation in the knowledge of him* (1:17).

Perhaps most of the Ephesians felt marginalized and ostracized in the city they had once called home. Their needs were great. But what was the answer? Paul believed it was to know God. This is our highest privilege, and it is the only thing worth boasting about (*Jer.* 9:23–4). That is why in his various 'prison letters' Paul prays that his readers' knowledge of God will increase (*Phil.* 1:9; *Col.* 1:9–10; *Philem.* 6), for to know God is to know him as *the God of our Lord Jesus Christ, the Father of glory* (verse 17). Paul's burden was, in essence, the burden the Lord Jesus poured out to his Father in his great intercessory prayer for the church (*John.* 17:1ff.) before his arrest. Thus to know God through Christ is to experience eternal life (*John.* 17:4).

But how can we get to know God better? We need to receive *a spirit of wisdom and of revelation in the knowledge of him* (verse 17). The phrase *spirit of wisdom* echoes the expression used for the Holy Spirit in Paul's Greek Old Testament (called the Septuagint). He may well have used it here in that sense. This is the Spirit who anointed Jesus so that he grew in wisdom and knowledge (*Isa.* 11:2ff.; cf. *Luke* 2:52). Christ now sends him to us to share with us *wisdom and revelation.*

Here *revelation* means essentially the same as 'illumination'. Paul is not suggesting that Christians receive their own private revelation. Rather, the Spirit brings us to know, understand, and live in the light of the revelation God has made of himself in Christ and through the Spirit.

When spiritual sight is thus restored, we become like Elisha's servant. He was terrified by the sight of the enemy occupation of the hills surrounding Dothan – just as the Ephesians might well have felt terrorized by Satan's powers (and terrorism, whether from outside or inside the church, is one of the tactics he often uses). In answer to prayer the servant's eyes were opened. He saw beyond the visible to the invisible and was able to walk by faith and not by sight (*2 Kings.* 6:17*; 2 Cor.* 4:18). He received a *spirit of wisdom and of revelation in the knowledge of him* [God].

Should the apostle have prayed for something more practical than this? Paul did not pray in this way because of a lack of knowledge of the actual practical difficulties the Ephesians faced. Nor did he pray in these lofty terms simply because this was a circular letter. Since he had lived in Ephesus for an extended period of time (*Acts* 20:31), he could easily have prayed for specific people. But, like the Lord Jesus as he prayed for his disciples in their hour of greatest crisis, he saw to the heart of their need: that they might have the eyes of their hearts enlightened to know God (verse 18, cf. *John.* 17:1–26).

When we ask such a question we reveal much about our priorities. We think we can see what is really important; but we are short-sighted. We need spiritual eye surgery from the Spirit in order to be able to see clearly.

WHAT TO PRAY FOR AS WE OUGHT

It is right to pray that our Christian friends' health will improve, that our family will do well at school or work, get along with one another, that our missionaries will settle well and be able to cope with culture shock and with language school. But Paul's prayers go higher and stretch farther. Our fundamental need is to see our privileges; for unless we see how great they are we will neither desire to enter into them fully nor will we be able live in the light of them.

Before we turn to consider Paul's prayer in detail, perhaps the best thing to do is simply to join him in prayer for Christians we know, and for ourselves, making his words our own and asking:

> *God of our Lord Jesus Christ, the Father of glory,*
> *give us a spirit of wisdom and of revelation in the knowledge of you,*
> *having the eyes of our hearts enlightened,*
> *that we may know*
> *what is the hope to which you have called us,*
> *what are the riches of your glorious inheritance in the saints,*
> *and what is the immeasurable greatness of your power towards us who believe,*
> *according to the working of your great might*
> *that you worked in Christ when you raised him from the dead*
> *and seated him at your right hand in the heavenly places,*
> *far above all rule and authority and power and dominion,*
> *and above every name that is named,*
> *not only in this age but also in the one to come.*
>
> Amen, and Amen.

6

Hope and Riches

For this reason, because I have heard of your faith in the Lord Jesus and your love toward all the saints, [16]I do not cease to give thanks for you, remembering you in my prayers, [17]that the God of our Lord Jesus Christ, the Father of glory, may give you a spirit of wisdom and of revelation in the knowledge of him, [18]having the eyes of your hearts enlightened, that you may know what is the hope to which he has called you, what are the riches of his glorious inheritance in the saints, [19]and what is the immeasurable greatness of his power towards us who believe . . . (Eph. 1:15–19)

Paul's prayer is so general it could be used in any age, in any place, and by any Christian. But therein, like the prayers of many of the Psalms, lies its genius. He asks that the Ephesians will learn three things: (i) the hope of the divine calling; (ii) the riches of God's glorious inheritance in the saints; and (iii) the immeasurable greatness of his power towards us who believe.

What does it mean to pray this for ourselves and our fellow believers?

HOPE FOR THE FUTURE

Paul prays that the Ephesians will know *the hope to which we have been called.* Later he underlines that by nature the Ephesians – as Gentiles – had 'no hope' (2:12). They were not the recipients of the special covenant promises God had given to Abraham and his posterity. For them life was, at the end of the day, a hopeless business – the future a closed door beyond which nothing could be seen.

At their funeral services there could be little more than a clinging to the past, some small consolation in gratitude for good memories – but no light dawned on them from the future.

The same is true in our modern world, for all its bravado and increasing scorn of the Christian faith. The funerals of the faithless are often events of enclosed darkness and hopelessness. Some are marked by a false jollity, a defiant mask that thinly disguises the harsh realities of death. It cannot be worn for long. How often a Christian's funeral stands in marked contrast! In the midst of pain there comes an almost tangible sense of light and peace, a sense of victory; there is a future and a hope – even in the valley of deep darkness.

The *hope*, of which Paul speaks here, is not to be confused with wishful thinking. It is an assurance of the reality of what we have not yet fully experienced. It will not disappoint us. Why? How can we be so sure? Because the love of God has already been poured into our hearts through the Spirit (*Rom.* 5:5). The world of heavenly love, which is the future destiny of believers, is already ours! The Spirit who has poured it into us also indwells us as the guarantee of the final inheritance (1:14). Having him we have a confident expectation for the future.

Why does *the hope to which he has called you* hold such a priority in Paul's prayers for his friends? Because how we live the Christian life is in large measure determined by how we think about the future. Putting it another way, the purpose behind God's revelation about the future is to transform the way we live in the present.

This was certainly true of our Lord's teaching: knowing that he will come again should lead us to live each day in the light of his return and to treat others in the light of his final assessment of our lives (see, for example, *Matt.* 25:31–46).

We find the same emphasis in Paul's letters: even his prayer life is informed by the future. Because he knows that the Lord will return in glory and judgment, he prays that believers may live in a way that is 'worthy of his calling and may fulfil every resolve for good and every work of faith by his power' (*2 Thess.* 1:11). Similarly, Peter speaks about the final dissolving of all things and the creation of the new heavens and earth in the day of the Lord, and adds, 'Since all these things are thus to be dissolved, what sort of people ought you to be in lives of holiness and godliness . . . ' (*2 Pet.* 3:11).

The church has lost this sense of the practical implications of the hope of the gospel. Perhaps we have become weary of too much crystal ball gazing, suspicious of too many maps and charts about 'the end times', uncomfortable with so much speculation accompanied by so little practical life transformation.

If that is the case, it should not be too difficult to understand why this is the first thing for which Paul prays. We need to see the future clearly if we are to live in the present faithfully. For the truth is, Christians are never 'too heavenly minded to be any earthly use.' It is far more likely that we are little earthly use (in the sense of making little impact on the world in which we live) because we are too this-worldly minded, too much like it to be able to transform it.

The realization that our citizenship is in heaven encourages us to live in the world as those whose ultimate identity lies elsewhere (cf. *Col.* 3:3–4). Since the Ephesians have been raised with Christ, they are called to live the life of the future in the present. New life 'in Christ' was to be a reality while they were still 'at Ephesus'. As their eyes are opened to appreciate this hope, their lives will be secured in the midst of a city where dark powers seek to engulf them.

To this Paul now adds a second petition. Not only is hope theirs; they are rich. What they now need is to discover their wealth.

RICHES BEYOND CALCULATION

What does Paul mean when he now prays that the Ephesians will realize *the riches of his [God's] glorious inheritance in the saints* (verse 18)? Does this refer to (a) the inheritance which God has in us, or (b) the inheritance we have in him?

In the Old Testament, the people were regarded as the Lord's inheritance (e.g. *Psa.* 28:9; 33:12; 78:62, 71; most beautifully expressed in *Mal.* 3:16–17). In turn, the Promised Land was the inheritance he gave to them (*Exod.* 12:25).

However, Old Testament believers saw beyond the land to the Landlord – ultimately God himself was their inheritance. The land was a physical expression of the spiritual riches they possessed in him. This was true not only of Aaron and his descendants who had no land inheritance (cf. *Num.* 18:20*; Ezek.* 44:28), but ultimately also of all the people: the Lord was their 'portion' (*Psa.* 73:26; 119:57; 142:5).

Paul's reference could be either to the riches we have in God, or to the remarkable biblical revelation that God regards his people as his 'treasured possession' (*Mal.* 3:17). Since God's inheritance in us and our inheritance in him are really two sides of the same coin, either interpretation implies the other.

On balance perhaps we should understand Paul to be referring to the riches we have. Certainly earlier, in verse 11, *inheritance* referred to our blessings, and Paul's two other petitions refer to the blessings God gives to us. This seems to be confirmed in the parallel section of Colossians (written around the same time as Ephesians), where Paul speaks of 'the inheritance of the saints in light' (*Col.* 1:12).

But in either case why is it important that our eyes are opened to see this? Because seeing this brings us a deep sense of dignity and security. Dignity is ours because of the knowledge that we are treasured by the great God in whom our lasting treasure is to be found. Security is guaranteed by the knowledge that he guards those he treasures as well as the treasures which are theirs (cf. *1 Pet.* 1:3–5).

Think how much this would mean to the group in the church at Ephesus whose background lay in the dark arts. They once had been among the wealthy book-owners of the city, so much so that in their radical commitment to Christ they had burned their occult literature (*Acts* 19:19). Why did they not sell it and use the proceeds for evangelism? Because evil must be rooted out and destroyed.

Their public action was, however, tantamount to destroying both their influence and their inheritance. They abandoned their profession and its lucrative income. Were they now among the poor? Then 'blessed are you who are poor, for yours is the kingdom of God' (*Luke.* 6:20). They needed to know that there are lasting riches for those who count this world's riches 'as loss because of the surpassing worth of knowing Christ Jesus . . . ' (*Phil.* 3:8 – perhaps Paul himself had been disinherited as a result of his conversion?). Knowing the riches that were theirs in Christ was a substantial defence against the allurement of the riches of Ephesus.

Christians – then and now – must live without regrets, 'forgetting what lies behind' (*Phil.* 3:13). There is no greater incentive to do that than to realize that lasting wealth lies in the priceless treasure we have received from God.

He has given his Son for us.

7

The Power-full Church

Having the eyes of your hearts enlightened, that you may know what is the hope to which he has called you, what are the riches of his glorious inheritance in the saints, [19]and what is the immeasurable greatness of his power towards us who believe, according to the working of his great might [20]that he worked in Christ when he raised him from the dead and seated him at his right hand in the heavenly places, [21]far above all rule and authority and power and dominion, and above every name that is named, not only in this age but also in the one to come. [22] And he put all things under his feet and gave him as head over all things to the church, [23] which is his body, the fullness of him who fills all in all (Eph. 1:18–23).

Sometimes the first taste of the new order of reality in Christ can be so overwhelming that we think there cannot be much left to learn! We could hardly be more mistaken.

When we are born again we see only those elements in the gospel that have been held before our blind eyes. The miracle of the man whose eyes Jesus touched *twice* illustrates our situation and experience. Our eyes are opened, and we 'see men but they look like trees walking' (*Mark*. 8:22–26). This is indeed wonderful – to see a world of life from which we have been barred. But there is more – much more – to come! This new world into which we have been brought in Christ is endlessly rich in wonder. That is why Paul prays for the Ephesians – to whom he had already given virtually the equivalent of a degree-length course of instruction in the gospel![2] – that their

[2] See Acts 19:9–10, especially fn. 3 in the ESV, suggesting that Paul taught daily for five hours for two full years.

spiritual eyes will be opened yet wider to see what God has done for them in Christ. He has given them hope; he has provided them with a priceless inheritance.

Now Paul adds a third element to his petition.

POWER BEYOND MEASUREMENT

Many early Christians suffered financial ruin because of their faith in Christ (*Heb.* 10:34b). Doubtless the slogan 'money is power' was as true of first century Ephesus as it is of the great cities of the world today. But the Ephesian Christians were financially challenged and socially weakened. In Christ, however, great *power* is available to the weak.

Paul himself experienced spiritual strength being given to him in times of weakness. Indeed he taught that such strength can be discovered only in the context of weakness. So he learned to be content in privation and even to 'boast' in his weaknesses – not in and of themselves but because the Lord taught him that his 'power is made perfect in weakness' (*2 Cor.* 12:9–10).

So too, these young Christians, surrounded by occult powers, and perhaps especially conscious of the socio-political power of the Diana cult in Ephesus (cf. *Acts* 19:19,34) needed to know that the One who was in them was stronger than the one who is in the world (*1 John.* 4:4).

SECURE IN CHRIST

All Christians need to know this security, which is why the apostolic letters emphasise it. The form taken by the powers of this age may vary. The nature and degree of oppression they foster may differ; but the reality of their presence and hostility to the gospel is the same. That is why we need to have our eyes opened not merely to the general idea that our God has power, but to *the immeasurable greatness of his power towards us . . . according to the working of his great might.*

Paul spells out in detail the power-standard of which he is speaking. It has come to expression in (i) the resurrection of Christ, (ii) the exaltation of Christ, and (iii) the victory of Christ over all the powers throughout the space-time and material-spiritual continuum (verses 20–22).

We must avoid sliding over Paul's statements here, as ideas with which we are already very familiar ('Of course there was great power in his resurrection, exaltation and victory – we know that!'). His concern is that we know these realities in terms of their implications for our own lives.

i. For Paul the resurrection of Christ was not simply resuscitation; it was an act of transformation in which we now share (2:5). True, we are not yet resurrected bodily; but the resurrection power of God is already operative in us.

ii. Furthermore, to say that God has *seated him [Christ] at his right hand* is not merely a picturesque way of putting things. These words deliberately echo Psalm 110:1, a verse which the New Testament writers refer to, cite, or allude to on some thirty different occasions. Jesus, our Saviour, sits at the right hand of God, enthroned in majesty and power.

iii. The work of Christ as sacrificing priest is ended; now has begun the epoch in which his victory over death, sin and Satan is being worked out. He reigns. Indeed he towers over *all rule and authority and power and dominion, and above every name that is named, not only in this age but also in the one to come* (verse 21). There is no rule greater than Christ's; there is no authority that can thwart his purposes; there is no power that can withstand his; there is no dominion that can prevent his advance. That is true in the present age and also in the age to come.

Magnificent though this statement is, Paul has still to state his applicatory climax. Christ is all this not for his own glory alone, but *to the church* (verse 22). He reigns over all things, subdues all his enemies, withstands all sinister evil forces in the universe in order to safeguard and bless his chosen people.

Our Lord himself stated this principle at the end of his ministry, as he sent his apostles into the world to make disciples of the nations. He commissioned them on the basis of the cosmic authority which his Father had given him as the crucified and exalted Mediator: 'All authority in heaven and earth has been given to me.' He promised his guiding and guarding presence 'I am with you always, to the end of the age' (*Matt.* 28:18–20). As Abraham Kuyper[3] delighted to say, there is not a square inch of the world that Christ does not claim with the words 'This is mine.' And because of our union with him (*Eph.* 1:3ff.), to say that it is his is to say that it is ours (cf. *1 Cor.* 3:21–23).

The implication of this is life-changing. Those who belong to Christ enjoy ultimate safety and security. No weapon formed against us can prevail (*Isa.* 54:17).

The movement of thought here in Ephesians 1 parallels the ringing triumph of Romans 8:28–39. Nothing can separate us from the love of God in Christ! Security from the powers that molested us; victory over the darkness that engulfed us – this was the confidence the gospel gave to the Ephesians and now gives to us. After all, does not Christ care for his own 'body' (1:23; cf 5:29–30)? It is this very language to describe the church – the body of Christ – that Paul uses.

THE BODY OF CHRIST

The Ephesian believers are 'saints'. Paul has used other descriptions as well: 'chosen' (verse 4), 'adoption' (verse 5), 'inheritance' (verses 11, 14). Now they are described as Christ's *body*.

The idea that the church is the 'body of Christ' is so familiar that we sometimes forget that Paul is the only biblical author who employs it. Did Paul 'invent' it? Was it an idea that developed from his experience on the Damascus Road? Did the Lord's words 'why are you persecuting me?' on later reflection suggest to Paul an intimate connection between Jesus and the church, like the relationship between a person and his or her body? That picture had already been used in the secular world to describe how Roman society should function (the whole body needs each part, and so all the parts are mutually dependent).

We may never know exactly what prompted Paul to think of the church in this way. Later (in chapter four) he develops it in detail.

[3] Abraham Kuyper (1837–1920) was a minister, theologian, and Prime Minister of the Netherlands 1901–1905.

But here he makes the intriguing, even puzzling statement. Christ's church is *his body, the fullness of him who fills all in all* (1:23).

Christ 'fills all in all'. Strange though the expression is, Paul is essentially summing up what he has just been saying: Christ is the Lord of heaven and earth – there is nothing beyond his control, nothing outside of his presence, nothing of which he is not Master.

The letter to the Colossians (with its many interesting parallels to Ephesians), speaks of Christ as the Creator of all things (just as here he is described as the Lord of all things). As Creator, Christ is the One in whom 'all things hold together' and also the head of the body the church, the One in whom the fullness of God dwells (*Col.* 1:15–19).

Here then is a glorious description of Christ and his people: Creator and Conquering Lord, head of the church, filled with the fullness of God, filling all things, and ruling all things for the sake of this body which is his fullness. The church is the community which Christ, in whom God's fullness dwells, now indwells, filling it up, as it were, with his presence, flooding it with his grace, conforming it to his image until it is filled with his likeness.

This is what it means to be a member of the church! These are the privileges into which we enter by God's grace. We need our eyes opened to see how rich we are!

We live too often below the level of our privileges. Like mountaineers who reach high altitude we find it difficult to breathe in such rarefied atmosphere as this. Sadly we are tempted to descend to lower ground, where the climbing is more manageable for our spiritual lungs. But if we cease to climb, we will never see the glorious realities that await our vision. No wonder, then, if we remain short-sighted Christians. May God open our eyes to see!

8

Dead or Alive?

And you were dead in the trespasses and sins [2]in which you once walked, following the course of this world, following the prince of the power of the air, the spirit that is now at work in the sons of disobedience – [3]among whom we all once lived in the passions of our flesh, carrying out the desires of the body and the mind, and were by nature children of wrath, like the rest of mankind. (Eph. 2:1–3)

First-century Ephesus had a large population. No wonder, for it was the richest city in the most prosperous province of the Roman Empire. It housed one of the seven great wonders of the ancient world, the largest building constructed in the Greek Empire: the temple of Diana. Measuring two hundred and twenty five feet by four hundred and twenty five feet, it dominated the city.

Yet for some of the Ephesians all this now meant nothing. The gospel had come to their city. Spiritual revolution resulted: 'the word of the Lord continued to increase and prevail mightily' (*Acts* 19:20). Vociferous and violent opposition arose when the transforming power of the gospel began to dent the profits of the Diana Cult businesses.

On one never-to-be-forgotten day, an unstable crowd gathered in the theatre and for two hours chanted 'Great is Artemis [the Greek name for the goddess Diana] of the Ephesians' (*Acts* 19:34). The theatre was the size of a sports stadium; the sense of antagonism to Christ must have been tangible and terrifying.

Faced with such opposition to the gospel, it is remarkable that the church of Christ lasted for any length of time in Ephesus. But the Ephesian church – seemingly in danger of being swallowed up

– continued to stand after Paul's departure. Now he wanted to help them to see their place in God's overarching plan for the whole of history.

Paul has already explained God's overarching purpose: to unite everything under the Lordship of Jesus Christ his Son. Three major obstacles present themselves:

(i) the dark powers that hold the fallen cosmos in bondage;

(ii) the spiritual death that separates us from God;

(iii) the deep seated alienation that causes the disintegration of humanity.

In his description of the Lordship of Christ (1:19–23) Paul has already shown how God has dealt with these obstacles. Jesus IS Lord, exalted above everything natural and supernatural, earthly and heavenly, animate and inanimate.

This message was spreading swiftly throughout the Empire. Now the men who had 'turned the world upside down' (*Acts* 17:6) had come to the region of Ephesus. The power of God had been manifested. Many lives were turned the right way up! Paul has explained (in 1:15–23) how God had inaugurated this reversal in Christ; now he begins to explain how all this applied to the Ephesians.

THE HUMAN CONDITION

The Ephesians are now 'in Christ'. Beforehand they were outside of Christ. They were not 'in Christ' but 'in Adam' (*1 Cor.* 15:22, cf. *Rom.* 5:12–21).

He now spells out in detail what this meant. The Ephesians had been alive physically: they breathed, they walked, they exercised daily choices. But in fact they were spiritually *dead*. They were 'in' *trespasses and sins* (verse 1) and *disobedience* (verse 2) – the living dead, the mortal living.

Paul's language here heightens the tension and drama of what he says. He postpones the main verb in his sentence until verse 5 ('God . . . made us alive'). The first four verses provide a litany of the hopeless and helpless condition in which we find ourselves apart from God's grace.

We were spiritually dead when we thought we were alive. No one thinks of him or her self as dead – certainly not 'dead' towards God! After all, we are able to think about God, assess him, judge whether we believe he exists or not. Furthermore, our lives – albeit not perfect – at least are 'above average'.

Such self-deception is a basic human trait. Apparently the vast majority of people believe they are 'better than average' drivers. In the nature of the case less than fifty per cent actually are! Many are self-deceived.

In the far more important realm of our spiritual condition, such self-deception is one of the major symptoms of spiritual death. We *walked* in *trespasses and sins* (2:1–2). We did not realize we were in the valley of the shadow which spiritual death casts. If we feared no evil it was because we did not realize that we were already held captive in the land of deep darkness.

A skilled mortician is able to present a dead body in a life-like fashion – even in a familiar and relaxed pose. Yet no life is present and no communication is possible. The same is true spiritually. A double mortal sickness has destroyed all hope of life: *trespasses* – acts of rebellion and rejection springing from a heart that is antagonistic by nature to God; and *sins* – the failures that infest our lives, concentrated in our failure to glorify and love God (*Rom*. 3:23). There is no spiritual health in us. We are worse than sick; we are *dead* (2:1).

Yes, acknowledges Paul, we *walked* (2:2). But just as we were the living dead, so we were also walking prisoners. All our exercise was within the confines of a prisoner-of-war camp! We were helpless followers of the one who had chained and bound us. That bondage is threefold, as the *Revised Standard Version* translation brings out (2:2–3):

Following the course of this world
Following the prince of the power of the air
Following the desires of body and mind

We were by nature enslaved to the world, the devil, and the flesh, in various ways showing that we were 'dedicated followers of fashion'. An exclusively horizontal world-and-life view with its value-system dominated our thinking – either engulfing us, or fascinating us. At the very least it plagued us inwardly so that we were constantly attracted, as if by a magnet, to find our deepest satisfaction in things that are transient.

PRISONERS OF WAR

Paul says we were also ensnared by the *prince of the power of the air* (2:2). The reference is, of course, to the Devil. Spiritual conflict is ultimately personal. Christ is not opposed merely by inanimate forces, but by living beings with dispositions hostile to his purposes – and especially by one many-named being, Satan, the Evil One, the Devil. Paul notes two things here about the Evil One.

(i) He is a *prince . . . spirit*. The language suggests authority and superiority. Satan is not a physical being with physical limitations. While he does not exercise ultimate authority, Paul does call him *the prince of the power of the air*. He is 'the god of this age' (*2 Cor.* 4:4, NIV). But he is no longer the ruler of the earth. That was originally man's domain, the place where Adam was called to exercise dominion, and over which Christ has reclaimed dominion for him (*Matt.* 28:18–20). Nor is heaven his throne, since there God alone reigns. Satan in fact is a wanderer, a Cain-like nomad (cf. *Gen.* 4:12). He roams the earth seeking to do his malevolent and destructive work.

(ii) He is *at work in the sons of disobedience* (a typical Hebrew way of saying 'those characterized by disobedience'). Here Paul summarizes what Scripture elsewhere teaches us more dramatically. Satan is *now at work*. He is always active.

Satan restlessly roves to and fro throughout the earth, hungering to satisfy his appetite to do God and his people ill, hating God and, when he finds a faithful saint, plotting to accuse and destroy him (cf. *Job* 1:7; 2:2). He 'prowls around like a roaring lion, seeking someone to devour' (*1 Pet.* 5:8). Unsatisfied restlessness and concentrated purpose combine with the mercilessness of the speed and power of his lion-like activity.

Paul had seen this often enough. He could recall the effect of such activity earlier in his own life. With restless spirit and single-minded focus he himself had done the Devil's work. He had encountered it later in the opposition that arose to his own preaching of Christ – all over the ancient world people had been stirred up by a hidden hand to oppose the message of grace and salvation in the Saviour who was 'meek and gentle' (cf. *2 Cor.* 10:1). How Satan must hate the goodness of God! He refused to trust it himself and so he engenders opposition towards it.

Paul uses plain terms here to speak of our sinful condition. The problem is not that our personalities have suffered at the hands of parents, or society, or genes. The truth is that we are spiritual rebels, guilty of moral and spiritual treason. We refuse God's 'Godness' and turn our backs on his goodness. We are, indeed, prisoners in darkness.

But Paul is not finished. It is one thing to be *'sons of disobedience'*. Worse is to follow. We are also *by nature children of wrath* (2:3). Sinister powers have mastered us. But more, indeed worse, is to come, as we shall see in what follows.

There is great joy in grace. But Paul knows that the only way we can be brought to appreciate it is if we first understand why we need it so much. The gospel he preached sobers us before it satisfies us.

9

Children of Wrath?

And you were dead in the trespasses and sins [2]*in which you once walked, following the course of this world, following the prince of the power of the air, the spirit that is now at work in the sons of disobedience –* [3]*among whom we all once lived in the passions of our flesh, carrying out the desires of the body and the mind, and were by nature children of wrath, like the rest of mankind.* (Eph. 2:1–3)

Dead, yet *walking*; *following*, yet in bondage to *the prince of the power of the air* – this was our natural condition. We were among the *sons of disobedience*. But there is a third dimension to human bondage: we *once lived in the passions of our flesh*.

Almost imperceptibly Paul has made an interesting shift in the pronouns he uses. '*You [Ephesians] were dead . . . you [Ephesians] once walked*' (verse 2). But then: *among whom we all once lived . . .* (verse 3). *We* all? Paul also?

How could this be a description of Paul? Elsewhere he writes: 'If anyone else thinks he has reason for confidence in the flesh, I have more: circumcised on the eighth day, of the people of Israel, of the tribe of Benjamin, a Hebrew of Hebrews; as to the law, a Pharisee; as to zeal, a persecutor of the church; as to righteousness, under the law blameless' (*Phil.* 3:4–6). How could this man, so zealous for the law, identify himself with people living *in the passions of our flesh*?

Paul himself provides the answer. He implies that he once had 'confidence in the flesh'. But to have confidence in the flesh *is* to be in bondage. For God has decreed that no flesh should glory in his presence (*1 Cor.* 1:29).

LIFE IN THE FLESH

The word *flesh* can refer to the physical body. But Paul uses it in a broader, more sinister sense here and elsewhere to refer to the human condition weakened and distorted by sin. It refers to the orientation of our whole being in a God-rejecting manner. The flesh is not an appendage to our existence. Rather it is the atmosphere in which we live, the air that we breathe in and out, and the fundamental alienated-from-God disposition of our inner being. The *flesh* is life turned in on itself without having the resources on which to live as we were intended – for the glory of God.

Thus, when Paul speaks about having 'reason for confidence in the flesh' his words carry a twofold nuance. He had reason to trust in his own ability, because it came to powerful expression in his persecution of the church. If anyone was a zealous Jew it was Saul of Tarsus! But now these same words constitute an open confession that he was as much a spiritual prisoner as any Gentile unbeliever: *we all once lived in the passions of our flesh*.

The essence of living in the passions of our flesh is such flesh-centred confidence. In Saul's life there was a literal fulfilment of his later words: 'while we were living in the flesh, our sinful passions . . . were at work in our members to bear fruit for death' (*Rom.* 7:5).

Thus while we tend to think of *the flesh* being in us, the more basic reality is that we are 'in the flesh' (cf. *Rom.* 7:5; 8:8–9). This is a world-order, an all-encompassing reality. And those who belong to that order (indeed, are imprisoned by it) have their minds attuned to it, dominated by it, focused on it. They 'live according to the flesh' and 'set their minds on the things of the flesh' thus expressing hostility to God (*Rom.* 8:5, 7).

When Paul describes sins that mark the flesh he includes physical activities but does not limit himself to them. Thus here he speaks of *the desires of* both *body and mind*. Flesh is intellectual as well as physical.

Elsewhere Paul uses an horticultural metaphor to describe living in the flesh. To live in this way is to sow to the flesh (*Gal.* 6:8) and leads to a harvest of the 'works of the flesh' (*Gal.* 5:19). These include: 'enmity, strife, jealousy, fits of anger, rivalries, dissensions . . . envy' as well as 'sexual immorality, impurity, sensuality'. So radically opposed are these to Christ's reign and to the fruit of the Spirit, that they have no place in the life-style of the kingdom of God. Those who are characterized by them cannot be breathing kingdom-cleansed air (*Gal.* 5:19–21) since 'those who belong to Christ Jesus have crucified the flesh with its passions and desires' (*Gal.* 5:24. Notice that Paul here refers to something Christians have done already. Not to have crucified the flesh with its passions is not to be a Christian!).

CHILDREN OF WRATH

The truth about the universal human condition is that in our sin we have fallen short of the glory of God (*Rom.* 3:23). But there is a further dimension to this tragedy. We have a yet more serious problem: God himself!

As Christians we are comforted by the thought that 'if God is for us, who can be against us?' (*Rom.* 8:32). But what if the reverse is the truth? What if God is not for us? What if God is against us? Then it matters little who is for us; we are in eternal danger.

This is what Paul means when he says that we are *by nature children of wrath*. This phrase, like 'sons of disobedience' (2:2), is a Hebrew way of saying 'marked by', 'characterized by', or 'destined for' – in this instance 'destined to experience the wrath of God'.

Wrath is the settled hostility of God's holy will towards everything that rebels against him. God does not 'fly off the handle' as we do, in a fit of rage. No, the terrible element in God's wrath is that besides being perfectly controlled it is totally concentrated, absolutely just, completely holy.

Paul does not raise his voice, or use capital letters, or underline words here. He is solemnized and subdued by what he knows: there is a future day of wrath (*Rom.* 2:5; *Col.* 3:6; *1 Thess.* 1:10; *Rev.* 6:16–17). The indication of its certainty is that God's wrath is already a present reality revealed from heaven (*Rom.* 1:18).

Wrath is a much-despised concept today. Those who live in ungodliness and unrighteousness often claim that there is no evidence of the terrible divine judgment about which the Bible speaks. They sin to their hearts' contentment, and walk away with impunity!

Not so, says Paul. These very behaviour patterns reveal them to be *children of wrath like the rest of mankind.* Their lifestyles actually constitute the biblical evidence that they already live under the wrath of God (cf. *John* 3:36). The very fact that they 'enjoy' license to live as they do is an evidence of the present manifestation of God's wrath. It proves the truth of Paul's words: God 'gave them up . . . to impurity . . . God gave them up to dishonourable passions . . . God gave them up to a debased mind' (*Rom.* 1:24, 26, 28). God's wrath is first of all revealed not in spectacular ways, but in the abandonment of sinners to themselves and to the unrestrained consequences of their actions. They sin as they please, but do not know or understand the message God is thus providentially sending them.

The problem of sin is not educational but ethical. Men may be given the most rigorous training for the élite corps of a military force, be able to withstand cruel torture – and yet perpetrate the deepest cruelties and be involved in the basest of obscenities. An athlete may exercise extraordinary control over his or her body for the purposes of competition, only to display by cheating, by sexual immorality, or in other ways that he or she is in bondage to the flesh. What is called 'freedom' is in fact licence. And licence is simply disguised bondage.

TAKING IT ALL IN

It is one thing for us to see that the gospel warns us about the wrath of God; it is another thing for us to be able to take it in. Paul's teaching here is that sin is all-pervasive in each of us, endemic in our very nature, and has spread throughout the human race (cf. *Rom.* 5:12–21). Our world has lived through the cruellest and most destructive of all centuries, our western civilization has undergone a moral disintegration of an astonishing kind – and yet we seek to retain the belief that wrath is an extreme idea.

Paul, by contrast, rightly sees that God cannot truly love unless he is also able to hate that which rebels against his love, refuses to receive, appreciate and enjoy it, and seeks to destroy its fruit. Reject his love in Christ and only wrath remains (*John.* 3:36). If we believe ourselves to be immune, or the apostle's words to be extreme it is because we have not realized the seriousness of sin. We have viewed it through the opaque lenses of the eyes of the flesh, not from the perspective of the holiness of God before whom the seraphim veil their faces.

The Book of Revelation gives us one of Scripture's most vivid pictures of this. On the day of the Lord 'the kings of the earth and the great ones and the generals and the rich and the powerful, and everyone, slave and free, hid themselves in the caves and among the rocks of the mountains, calling to the mountains and rocks, "Fall on us and hide us from the face of him who is seated on the throne, and from the wrath of the Lamb, for the great day of their wrath has come, and who can stand?"' (*Rev.* 6:15–17).

As we try to take this in, we need to remember that we all must appear before Christ the Lamb to receive what we deserve for what we have done, whether good or ill (*2 Cor.* 5:10). Paul taught this consistently, believed it implicitly, and lived in the light of it. If we are to engage in gospel-centred evangelism we need to have the shadow of the wrath of God in divine judgment touch our spirits.

It is a sobering thing to believe the gospel and to see that the goodness of the good news is integrally related to solemn divine judgment. It is a glorious thing to know that Jesus delivers us; but it is so only when we realize that what he delivers us *from* is 'the wrath to come' (*1 Thess.* 1:10).

10

But God

But God, being rich in mercy, because of the great love with which he loved us, [5]even when we were dead in our trespasses, made us alive together with Christ – by grace you have been saved – [6]and raised us up with him and seated us with him in the heavenly places in Christ Jesus, [7]so that in the coming ages he might show the immeasurable riches of his grace in kindness towards us in Christ Jesus. (Eph. 2:4–7)

The sentence that follows Paul's introductory greeting in chapter 1 is – as we saw – remarkable for its length. The opening statement in chapter 2 is equally remarkable – but this time because of its lengthy delay of a main verb. At last it appears in the middle of verse five: *But God . . . made us* [who were 'dead in our trespasses'] *alive together with Christ*. Paul's language is even more arresting than it appears in English where the words *together with* are separate from the verb 'make alive'. In Greek they form a prefix to the verb itself. Translated in a literal way Paul says: 'God together-gave-life with Christ.'

THE SOURCE OF NEW LIFE

Paul's point is clear. We were *dead*. But by contrast with our deserts God gave us new life in Christ.

To a biblically instructed ear, the phrase *But God* is reminiscent of the turning points of the personal or corporate laments in the Psalms. Psalm 41 is an example. David is surrounded by the malice of enemies and experiences the betrayal of a close friend. As he focuses on his situation the outlook is bleak and he can see no way out. Then he looks up to the throne of heaven. By faith he sees God himself seated on it and cries out, '*But you, O Lord . . .*' He begins to realize that if God is for him nothing, ultimately, can be against him (*Psa.* 41:1–13).

Similarly the heart-rending cries of Psalm 102:1–11 pour out the author's sense of desolation and affliction. Then, in a moment of illumination his gaze is lifted beyond his circumstances. Above his chaos he sees the Sovereign Lord. And so he sings: '*But you, O Lord*, are enthroned for ever . . .' (*Psa.* 102:12).

Again, in Psalm 130 (a 'Pauline Psalm' as Luther acutely observed) the author is overwhelmed by a sense of sin. Who could ever stand before a holy God? 'If you, O Lord, should mark iniquities, O Lord, who could stand?' His situation is helpless and hopeless. Then he regains a focus on God: '*But with you* there is forgiveness . . .' (*Psa.* 130:3–4).

What prompts such deliverance and relief?

WHAT GOD HAS DONE

We are not merely dysfunctional or sick; we are spiritually dead. God does for us what we cannot do either for ourselves or for one another. By his Spirit he united us to Christ (Paul will explain how in verses 8–10). He *made us alive*; *he raised us up*; he *seated us with him* at his right hand (verses 5–7; cf. 1:20).

Earlier Paul had described how God has dealt with the guilt of our sin through Christ. Through Christ's shed blood we enjoy forgiveness (1:7). But we need more than forgiveness. A. M. Toplady was right to teach us to sing:

> 'Be of sin the double cure,
> Cleanse me from its *guilt and power*'.[1]

So here Paul underlines that the death of Christ and our pardon cannot be separated from the resurrection of Christ and our liberation. These are two sides of a single coin.

The story of Lazarus provides a powerful illustration. Although

[1] From the hymn 'Rock of Ages, cleft for me'.

he was dead and therefore deaf, Christ announced good news (gospel) to him: 'Lazarus come forth'. Although he was dead and bound in grave clothes, Christ made him alive (*John.* 11:43; cf. *Eph.* 2:6). Christ raised him from the tomb. Soon Lazarus was freed from the clothes of sin and death (*John.* 11:44; cf. *Eph.* 2:6); Later, having completed this great work, Christ sat down and shared table fellowship with him (*John.* 12:2; cf. *Eph.* 2:7).

So it is with us. What Christ did physically for Lazarus through his word and by the power of the Spirit he continues to do spiritually for us by the same instruments. Salvation thus involves both pardon for our sins and new life. One without the other would not be the complete good news we really need. But now, united to Christ we have been raised up from spiritual death. We see the kingdom, we love his Word, and we experience life in God's family.

But there is more! We are united to a risen, ascended and enthroned Christ, and therefore we already share in his triumph. This is what Paul means by our being *seated* with Christ *in the heavenly places*. That descriptive language echoes Psalm 110:1, as did Paul's earlier statement about Christ himself (1:20). Along with the forgiveness of our sins (1:7) comes deliverance from bondage to the dark powers we once followed (2:2). For, the Christ with whom we are united is seated in triumph 'above all rule and authority and power and dominion, and above every name that is named, not only in this age but also in the one to come. And he put all things under his feet . . .' (1:21, 22).

The implication of these majestic words corresponds to Paul's triumphant statement in Romans 8:37: 'We are more than conquerors through him who loved us'. If God is for us in Christ in this way – who then can be against us? The answer? Ultimately, no one!

WHY HAS GOD DONE IT?

In one sense, of course, the reason for this is inexplicable. When we ask why God has done this we tend to be looking for reasons, explanations, even qualifications we can find in ourselves. But Paul insists that God has done this simply because he is a gracious God working out his own holy will. Salvation depends 'not on human will or exertion, but on God, who has mercy' (*Rom.* 9:16). Notice

Paul's exuberant characterization of God: *rich in mercy . . . great love with which he loved us . . . immeasurable riches of his grace in kindness towards us* (2:4, 7). Here, as elsewhere, the apostle lingers long and lovingly on the thought of God's amazing goodness to those who have not only forfeited it but merit his just condemnation. His mercy is *rich*, his love *great,* his *kindness* immeasurably gracious!

Two things should be noted here.

The first is that our salvation is dependent on the work of Christ. God *made us alive* in Christ, *seated us* with Christ and displays *his grace in kindness* towards us through Christ.

Secondly, in underlining this, we should not fall into the error of thinking that the love, grace, and kindness of God are the *result* of the work of Christ. The reverse is the case – as Paul's letters everywhere teach. God shows, or demonstrates, his prior love for us in Christ's death (*Rom.* 5:8).

The gospel truly reveals the deepest heartbeat of God towards us. Jesus' work did not – nor did it need to – persuade an angry Father to love his wayward children. The atonement is not a form of inner-trinitarian blackmail. No: the Father loved us and did not spare his own Son for our salvation (*Rom.* 8:32); the Son loved us, and 'did not count equality with God a thing to be grasped . . .' (*Phil.* 2:6); the Spirit loved us (*Rom.* 15:30) and is not ashamed to indwell and sanctify us.

Why should it be so important for Paul to emphasize this? Because we can misinterpret 'the gospel' message to mean that God loved us *because* Christ died for us, as if the sheer amount of suffering he experienced made the Father relent of his hatred towards us and now begin to love us and be kind to us.

Our spiritual forefathers used to speak about the way Christians 'live below the level of their privileges'. This is a case in point. If only we would settle our hearts on what the apostle says here about the character of God! Think about these three statements – they merit a lifetime of meditation:

1. God is *rich in mercy.*
2. God has *loved us* with *great love.*

3. God has shown kindness to us which expresses the *immeasurable* (the word is the root of our word 'hyperbole') *riches of his grace in kindness towards us in Christ Jesus.*

How wonderful, then, that Paul combines together the lavish love displayed in Christ with the ultimate purposes of God. For *in the coming ages* he means to *show the immeasurable riches of his grace in kindness towards us in Christ Jesus* (2:7). Our blessing and God's displaying his glory are not antithetical – as though the glory of God could only be displayed at our expense (is this what we fear?). No, God's glory is best seen in the underserved and unexpected character of what he has done for us in Christ. The effect of that in our lives will shine out of God's display cabinet for all eternity.

We understand and appreciate this only partially. But a day will dawn when the whole universe will witness the unveiling of what God has really done. Then all things will bow at the name of Jesus and every tongue will confess that he is Lord. And all creation, *as worshippers* in the temple of the Lord will call out 'Glory!' (*Psa.* 29:9).

11

Grace Works

For by grace you have been saved through faith. And this is not your own doing; it is the gift of God, [9]not a result of works, so that no one may boast. [10]For we are his workmanship, created in Christ Jesus for good works, which God prepared beforehand, that we should walk in them. (Eph. 2:8–10)

Salvation – forgiveness and freedom – is the goal of the gospel. But it is not the only goal, nor is it the ultimate goal. For, 'the chief end of man' is 'to glorify God and to enjoy him for ever'. The ultimate goal of our salvation must be his glory and our enjoyment of him. This is what we are saved for.

Paul has already made this clear. Christ is exalted above all things (1:20–23). God has also raised us up from spiritual death to triumphant life in Christ (2:1–6). His goal in doing so is that 'in the coming ages he might show the immeasurable riches of his grace' (2:7). Always in view is the glory of the author of salvation whom we have come to know and enjoy.

But this strong emphasis in Ephesians chapters 1 and 2 on the sovereign activity of God raises a question. If salvation begins in God's eternal election and is effected by what Christ has done – not by us – so that salvation is *by grace* – where does our activity fit in? If God saves us sovereignly, graciously, without our contribution, is there no need for faith or, for that matter, for conversion and repentance?

Paul gives an immediate explanation. Yes, we are saved by God's sovereign grace. But that grace is received in Christ *through faith* (2:8). Surely, then, we do contribute something to our salvation – faith? 'No', responds Paul, *this is not your own doing; it is the gift of God.* Faith is indeed our response, but it is not our contribution!

Even in English, however, Paul's words *(By grace you have been saved through faith. And this . . .)* raise two important questions.

THE REFERENCE POINT

To what does *this* refer? There are several possibilities:

- Faith,
  or
- Salvation ('you have been saved'),
  or
- Grace,
  or
- All of the above – being saved by grace through faith

To what does 'this' refer in the words 'and this is not your own doing'? The pronoun *this* is neuter (in Paul's Greek). But its possible antecedents (the word or words to which it refers) – 'faith', 'salvation' ('you have been saved') and 'grace' are all *feminine* in gender in Greek!

Paul may actually be thinking about the whole previous statement: being saved by grace through faith. But it is possible that while *this* is neuter it could refer back to grace, or salvation, or faith – all of which are 'neuter gender' realities even although in Greek grammar they are grammatically feminine words!

- Does *this* refer to *grace*? By definition grace is not our own doing. Why then speak of grace as the gift of God? This view suggests that Paul's statement would be redundant.
- Does *this* refer to 'salvation'? Since it is by *grace* it would, again, be redundant to say it is a *gift*. The same would be true of the view that Paul is taking here of the entire phrase.

Paul does, however, use 'redundant' language for emphasis in a similar context in Romans 3:24: we 'are justified by his *grace* as a *gift*'. So these two views cannot be absolutely ruled out.

- Does *this* refer to *faith*? It is the immediate antecedent, and therefore perhaps the most likely reference. If it is this Paul refers to, then the flow of thought would then seem to go like this:

By grace you have been saved through faith
So, yes, faith is active – but

faith itself is the work of grace
it is not your own doing.

In fact this faith is a gift of God;

it is not effected by your works;
if it were, you would be able to boast.
That is something you cannot ever do.

It may not be possible to be dogmatic here. In any case, later in Ephesians Paul indicates that faith is a gift from God. He prays for 'peace . . . love and faith *from God the Father and the Lord Jesus Christ*' to be experienced by the church (*Eph.* 6:23).

WHO BELIEVES?

Whether Ephesians 2:8 is interpreted in the narrow or broad sense, it suggests that faith is given to us by God. But God does not do the believing for us. *We* are the ones who must believe!

Think here of Paul's illuminating words to the Philippians, 'It has been granted to you that for the sake of Christ you should not only believe in him but also suffer for his sake . . . ' (*Phil.* 1:29). Faith is 'granted' (i.e. gifted in grace) to us just as is suffering. But this gift of suffering means *we*, not God, experience the suffering: we suffer! In the same way God 'gives' faith; but he does not do the believing; we do.

The gospel calls for a faith response. That faith is our activity. But it is not 'in us' by nature to believe. Faith needs to be effected in us by God. In that sense it is his *gift*.

The genius of God's plan of salvation is that he has devised a means by which we are actively engaged in faith, and yet contribute nothing towards salvation. It is a free gift to which faith adds nothing. Salvation is all, and always, of *grace*. It is never resourced in what

I am by nature; it is not dependent on my *works*. It comes from God; therefore no one who has it can boast about it! This is divine genius indeed!

THE LORD'S HANDIWORK

Rather than working for our own salvation we are in fact God's *workmanship*. Does this mean that we can be indifferent to holiness? On the contrary, *we are . . . created in Christ Jesus for good works* – and these are the *good works, which God prepared beforehand, that we should walk in them* (2:10).

There is a beautiful spiritual balance here. Faith is a gift, yet we exercise it. Good works do not save, yet we cannot be saved without beginning to *walk in* the *good works, which God prepared beforehand.* Even the idea that good works constitute something we 'walk in' is intriguing. It suggests an entirely new lifestyle.

Notice the parallel ideas Paul has presented in verses 7 and 10. God has saved his people:

verse 7: So that they might be a visible display of his grace towards us in Christ.
verse 10: So that they might exhibit in their lives God's workmanship.

Paul has more to say about the ways in which God displays his glory in the church. It is to be, as it were, a working model of his saving power and grace. Heaven may be the final showroom; but here on earth God is already 'showing what he can do.'

The church triumphant is an art gallery where God displays reflections of his glory. It is a portrait gallery in which the family likeness is seen in countless different individuals who together display his infinite glory.

The church visible, here and now, is a workshop. The Divine Artist is still painting his likeness on the canvas of our lives; the Divine Potter still has the clay in his hands.

The time for the final exhibition has not yet come. But one day it will. Then all that God has done in us in secret, invisible to the naked eye, will become visible for all to see.

What a day that will be!

12

Past Division

Therefore remember that at one time you Gentiles in the flesh, called 'the uncircumcision' by what is called the circumcision, which is made in the flesh by hands – [12]*remember that you were at that time separated from Christ, alienated from the commonwealth of Israel and strangers to the covenants of promise, having no hope and without God in the world.* (Eph. 2:11–12)

God has revealed his secret purposes in Christ. He has planned the restoration of a fallen and fragmented creation. While he gave hints of his plan in the Old Testament period, it is only now, in Christ, that the mystery – hidden in the heart of God in eternity – has been revealed.

Paul will say more about this in chapter 3. But first he addresses another part of the evidence that God is now bringing his purposes to pass.

Three major obstacles oppose God's 'summing up' everything in Christ: the sinister powers that have usurped dominion in this world; the lost spiritual condition of the human race; the deep seated alienations that exist among people in the world.

In particular, Paul realized that if God were to fulfil his plan to unite everything under Christ then the long-standing barrier between Jew and Gentile would need to be broken down.

Ephesians 2:11–22 now shows how God's grace works in a community way. Paul moves from using the second person to the first person, from 'you' to 'we'. He is not simply distinguishing here between the Ephesians ('you') and himself and his companions ('we'), but between the Ephesians *as Gentiles* and himself and his companions *as Jews*. He describes what they were without Christ, what God has done for them through Christ, and what they are becoming in Christ.

After thirty-three verses of indicative statements, we now come to Paul's first imperative: *Therefore remember . . . remember*. Apart from the implied imperative in 3:13 ('I ask you not to lose heart' = 'Don't lose heart!'), no further exhortation appears until 4:1. The entire first half of Ephesians is, for all practical purposes, an 'imperative-free zone'!

It is a healthy exercise to ask ourselves if we share Paul's emphasis in understanding and communicating the gospel. Its imperatives ('believe', 'repent') always depend on the prior indicatives of God's grace. Always! Confuse indicative and imperative and we cease to use the grammar of the gospel; eventually what we believe and communicate will cease to be gospel (good news) and become moral lecture ('do this').

But what are the Ephesians (and we also) to remember? The verses that follow take us through three stages:

1. What we Gentiles were without Christ (verses 11–12).
2. What God has done for us through Christ (verses 13–18).
3. What we are now becoming in Christ (verses 19–22).

WITHOUT CHRIST

In verses 1–10 Paul had described our lost condition from the viewpoint of our personal depravity. Now he views it from the perspective of redemptive history.

God has never left himself without a witness (*Acts* 14:17). In addition to the testimony of the created order (*Psa*. 19:1; *Rom*. 1:18ff.; *Acts* 17:22ff.), he revealed himself in history, especially in the calling of Abraham and the creation of a covenant community. That community was the unique context for and vehicle of God's special saving revelation to the world. He called his people to be a light to the nations, a testimony to the only true and living God and to his saving grace. The men in the nation had a physical mark on their bodies by which God said to them 'Remember my covenant; live as my people.'

The Ephesians were excluded by birth from covenant privileges (cf. *Rom.* 9:4–5 for Paul's listing of them). They were *Gentiles in the flesh* – they had no badge of God's covenant on them and were excluded from his people. They were despised as *uncircumcised* by those who did have the covenant mark – even although they themselves were spiritually uncircumcised and therefore were not true covenant children (cf. *John.* 8:39ff.).

Because the Ephesians had no natural access to God's special revelation, they did not share the privileges of God's people: they were separated from Messiah, alienated from the covenant community (*the commonwealth of Israel,* verse 12), and were strangers to God's covenant promise (they did not belong to the 'seed' to whom the promises were made). They were *without God*, and therefore had *no hope.* How could they have *hope* when they had no future grace to look forward to and anticipate?

By nature, then, we were Christless, stateless, friendless, Godless, hopeless; in a nutshell, 'not God's people' (cf. *1 Pet.* 2:10). Thus if Ephesians 2:1–10 underscored the helplessness of our condition, 2:11–22 underscores its hopelessness.

But why did Paul feel it was important to remind the Ephesians to *remember* this? Should they not rather 'forget' these things now that they were Christians and had entered into the blessing described in 1:4ff.? While he does not pause to answer that question here, it is answered in Romans 11:13ff. Both Jew and Gentile are prone to pride. We experience the grace of God but in our sinfulness begin to believe secretly that we were just the kind of people who merited it! Paul seeks to safeguard his friends against such spiritual amnesia.

We need this word of God echoing regularly in our minds. Remember who you were; do not forget where you came from; all that you have become, all the blessings you enjoy are entirely of God's grace. You did not receive them because you are the kind of person who would respond well to them. You are by nature a helpless and hopeless Gentile; furthermore you were outside of the orbit of God's people. You are what you now are only because of grace.

WHAT GOD HAS DONE

Paul's words 'But God . . .' marked the turning point of 2:1–10. In the second half of the chapter there is a similar turning point in the words '*But now . . .*' (2:13). In the unified, but multi-faceted, work of God's saving grace, he has not only raised us from spiritual death but also reversed our spiritual alienation. Once we were dead, now we live with Christ; once we were *far off*, now we have been *brought near*.

Notice, however, that while this being *brought near* lies at the root of the fellowship of Gentile with Jew, it is not primarily a horizontal, but a vertical transformation. It takes place *in Christ Jesus*, through the shedding of his *blood* that he might *reconcile us both to God in one body through the cross* (2:16). We are united to each other only because we are united to Jesus Christ.

Paul goes on to spell out the dimensions of this. But before we consider what he says we should pause to remember what we ourselves were, without Christ – and what would have become of us had God not been 'rich in mercy'. The epitaph on our spiritual tombstone might have read as follows:

Dead
Following the course of this world
Following the prince of the power of the air
Carrying out the desires of body and mind
By nature children of wrath
Uncircumcised
Separated from Christ
Alienated from the commonwealth of God's people
Strangers to the covenants of promise
Without hope
Without God

But now a new epitaph is possible:

Alive
Loved by God
Raised up with Christ
Seated in heavenly places
Recipient of divine kindness
Saved by grace
God's workmanship

Brought near
Reconciled
United with fellow believers
Enjoying access to God
Fellow citizen with the saints
Built into the temple of God

One or other epitaph will be yours. But which?

13

The Big Picture

But now in Christ Jesus you who once were far off have been brought near by the blood of Christ. [14]*For he himself is our peace, who has made us both one and has broken down in his flesh the dividing wall of hostility* [15]*by abolishing the law of commandments and ordinances, that he might create in himself one new man in place of the two, so making peace,* [16]*and might reconcile us both to God in one body through the cross, thereby killing the hostility.* (Eph. 2:13–16)

Sin is a multi-dimensional reality. The Bible therefore has a wide variety of words to describe it. It follows that the work of salvation needs to be multi-dimensional in character. That is why the New Testament also describes the work of Christ in several different ways.

Here, having described our sinful condition and explained our need as sinners, Paul underlines the four things Christ has done to bring us full salvation.

CHRIST MAKES PROPITIATION

Jesus died for our sins. We are brought near *by the blood of Christ.* This is the language of the temple and its sacrifices. People confessed their sins symbolically over an animal; the punishment for them was 'transferred' to the animal substitute, which was then slaughtered. The *blood* (= death) of the innocent One paid the penalty for the sin of the guilty. It bore the wrath of God.

The New Testament underlines that the blood of bulls and goats could never take away sins (*Heb.* 10:4). The very nature of the

Mosaic sacrificial system indicated that. The blood of an animal is an inadequate substitute sacrifice for the sins of a human.

Old Testament men and women of faith would have understood this. For the sacrifices were 'continually offered every year' yet those who made them still had a 'consciousness of sin' (*Heb.* 10:1, 2). Indeed the very fact that 'every priest stands daily at his service, offering repeatedly the same sacrifices' (*Heb.* 10:11) was evidence that the pardon promised by God was not actually provided by animal sacrifice. Otherwise the sacrifices would not have needed to be repeated.

But now the blood of Christ's violent death, in which he was 'like a lamb that is led to the slaughter' (*Isa.* 53:7), has fulfilled all the Old Testament patterns that pointed forward to the reality of a final and sufficient sacrifice for sins.

CHRIST BREAKS DOWN SEPARATION

Christ *himself is our peace.* Christ has made both Jew and Gentile one *in himself,* having *broken down in his flesh the dividing wall of hostility* (verse 14).

The reason Gentile believers were no longer 'outsiders' was not that the Jews had altered their feelings towards them, or that Gentiles had engaged in the Jewish ritual to make them more acceptable. No! Christ himself had brought Jew and Gentile together.

The Jewish believer has fellowship with God not on the basis of circumcision, national identity, possession of the torah (the law), making the Mosaic sacrifices, or access to the temple in Jerusalem, but in Christ alone. The scaffolding within which his forefathers lived has been dismantled; now only Christ stands before him as the fulfilment of circumcision and torah and sacrifice and temple! He enjoys a right relationship with God, the status of being God's son because through faith he is 'in Christ'.

Exactly the same is true for the Gentile believer who has no history or experience of circumcision, torah, sacrifice, or temple. But he or she has Christ, and in him every spiritual blessing. The Jewish believer longed for and has now received his inheritance through faith in Christ. Gentile believers have discovered it in exactly the same way!

This is why Paul stresses that it is Christ *himself* who *is our peace.*

CHRIST EFFECTS RECONCILIATION

Christ has *broken down in his flesh the dividing wall of hostility* between Jew and Gentile, *by abolishing the law of commandments and ordinances*. Perhaps at the back of Paul's mind here was the literal wall that separated the court of the Gentiles from the inner courts of the Jerusalem temple. For a Gentile to go beyond this carried an automatic death sentence.

Paul himself almost lost his life when he was suspected of bringing an uncircumcised Gentile – Trophimus, an Ephesian! – into the temple (*Acts* 21:27ff.). The Jews assumed he had taken him beyond this *dividing wall* that formed the perimeter fence of the Court of the Gentiles. It was about four feet six inches high and bore the ominous notice forbidding Gentile access: 'Whoever is arrested will himself be responsible for his death, which will follow'.

In the death of Jesus, that *dividing wall* has been demolished by God (cf. verse 18). Now in Christ Jew and Gentile share the 'court' of God. In fact, not only has that partition been broken down; the curtain that barred all access to the holiest place (save for the High Priest's entry once a year) has been torn in pieces (*Luke*. 23:45). The death of Christ effected the divine de-consecration of the Jerusalem temple, signalling its ultimate destruction in AD 70. His atoning sacrifice fulfilled the symbolism of everything that took place in the temple and thus brought about the abolition of the *law of commandments and ordinances* – that is, the whole Mosaic system under which Old Testament believers lived.

THE KEY IDEA

This is a key idea in Paul's understanding of the gospel. In a nutshell he sees God's dealings with his people as divided into two basic epochs – that of the First Man and First Adam and that of the Second Man and Last Adam (cf. *Rom*. 5:12–21; *1 Cor*. 15:45–49). The First Man, Adam, sinned and his sin led to curse, disintegration and death. The Second Man, Jesus, came to undo all that.

But what of the interim period between the First and Second Men? God preserved the world that deserved destruction through the covenant with Noah (*Gen*. 8–9). On the ground that he cleared through the flood, God began to rebuild what we might call a 'house of salvation'.

Stage one of his building programme involved calling a people out of the world through the covenant with Abraham (*Gen.* 12:1ff.). The Lord promised that the 'seed' (already prophesied in *Gen.* 3:15) would come and bring blessing to all the nations.

Stage two involved creating a temporary, interim 'home' for his people. So he brought them out of Egypt and placed them in a specific 'holy' land, commanded them to express a specific 'holy' lifestyle, and to meet with him in a specific 'holy' place by means of specific 'holy' rituals and sacrifices which portrayed his willingness to forgive them when they sinned and restore them to the blessings of his covenant love.

HOW TO UNDERSTAND THE LAW OF MOSES

But this second stage – instituted through Moses – was always intended to be an interim arrangement. The Mosaic ordinances pointed beyond their own epoch to their fulfilment in Christ. So Jesus taught that he fulfilled the law (*Matt.* 5:17–20). Thus the Mosaic law that was *an interim arrangement for a specific people group in a particular place for a limited time* was brought to an end in Christ. Christ thus brought it to an end. In that sense, Moses is no more!

This sounds so radical that it is perhaps not surprising that like Stephen before him (*Acts* 6:11, 14) Paul was accused of overthrowing and destroying the law (*Acts* 21:21). But that very fact suggests that we are on the right track in understanding what he is teaching here.

But we must also be patient enough to listen carefully to what Paul teaches and not jump to false conclusions.

The law of Moses was fulfilled in Christ (cf. *Matt.* 5:17–20; *Rom.* 10:4).

But there were elements in Moses' ministry that were not uniquely Mosaic. They belonged to God's original design and will for our lives. They had a particular form in the Moses epoch, but they embodied the permanent purposes of God.

This was obviously true of the Ten Commandments. This is why Paul can say that Christ has fulfilled the law and yet scatter references to the Ten Commandments throughout his letters! *For those commandments express God's original purpose for man at creation.*

Adam was created in such a way that the principles of the Ten Commandments were built into the moral engine that drove his existence. His life setting determined the *form* in which he received the commands, engraved within his very being as the image of God. He was created good, and lived in an unfallen world. God's will (law) was already written on his heart, in the very instincts by which his life was driven.

But Moses was given these same laws in a radically different context – for people in a fallen and sinful world. He was given the law the way we were given 'commandments' when we were children: a series of 'do not' commands that, in their own way, implied a series of 'do' commands. In a similar way God gave his people 'under age' (*Gal.* 4:3 cf. *Gal.* 3:24) eight negative commands. These, as Jesus taught, *implied* their positive opposites (cf. *Matt.* 5:21–48).

In fact God gave his people only two positive commands. The Sabbath commandment was one (although even it was boundaried by negative prohibitions), and the only commandment that lacks a negative – honouring parents. Interestingly, within God's covenant provisions, keeping these positively-expressed commandments would help even the children appreciate that the negative commandments enshrined positive implications.

Christ has fulfilled the law of Moses as a whole. He was fully obedient to its moral demands. He fulfilled its symbolism by himself being the sacrifice for our sins. God's new covenant people are now 'in Christ'. The scaffolding built in Moses' ministry is no longer necessary, since Christ, the true temple, has come. Indeed, to leave the administration of Moses in place would be to miss the whole point of it being established in the first place!

But God's purposes, expressed in a particular ('interim') form in the Ten Commandments, are not abolished. His moral law is all the more appropriate for those who are being transformed into the likeness of God (*Eph.* 4:24). What the law could not do because of the weakness of our flesh, God has done in Christ. The goal and result, however, was 'in order that the righteous requirement of the law might be fulfilled in us . . . who walk . . . according to the Spirit' (*Rom.* 8:4).

Paul brings this out in what follows:

CHRIST INAUGURATES A NEW CREATION

Christ's purpose is to *create in himself one new man (humanity) in place of the two* (verse 15). The early Christians were sometimes known as a 'third race of men' (Gentiles and Jews being the other two). Every imperative that Paul issues to the Ephesians depends on this reality: we are part of the new creation in Christ.

God created the original humanity in Adam. That humanity is destined for the outer darkness because of sin. God has now created a second humanity *within the world of the old humanity*. This was what he promised to Adam and Eve (*Gen.* 3:15) and to Abraham and his descendants (*Gen.*12:1ff.). This promised seed would be the origin of a final humanity, which would flow from the seed of Abraham.

The promised seed has now come – it is Jesus (cf. *Matt.* 1:1–17!). This seed fell into the ground and died (*John.* 12:24), but was raised again into the glory-life of resurrection. All those who are part of his family, by grace and faith, share in his new life. They constitute a new humanity – no longer the humanity of the first Adam, but that of the Last Adam, Jesus Christ.

In this new humanity, the hostility, which was created within the old humanity, has been transcended. The cross that killed Christ also marks with death everything that alienates one believer from another.

Divided (from God) we have fallen, Jew and Gentile alike. Neither Adam nor for that matter Moses can pardon our sins and give us new life (*Rom.* 8:3–4). But now through faith, united to Christ we stand. He has made *one new man in place of the two* (verse 15). Hostilities are ended (verse16). Christ gives us peace. In fact *he himself is our peace* (verse 14)!

14

But Now

And he came and preached peace to you who were far off and peace to those who were near. [18]*For through him we both have access in one Spirit to the Father.* (Eph. 2:17–18)

The Christian church is today composed mainly of Gentiles. It has been since the first century.

Ethnic division, hostility, and prejudice have always been present in the proud human heart. The division between Jew and Gentile in the ancient world displayed many complex manifestations of this. For Paul it was one of the wonders of the gospel that it was capable of dissolving this deep-seated alienation. It united Jews and Gentiles together in one new humanity in which they saw each other as brothers and sisters in Christ.

CHRIST OUR PEACE

The second half of Ephesians 2 deals with this new relationship established between Jews and Gentiles who have come to faith in Christ. Now both stand on the same ground at the foot of the cross, with nothing to contribute to their salvation (as Paul underlined in 2:1ff.). Christ has made the one true sacrifice that is effective for all the sins of all of his people. The temporary arrangements of the Mosaic system are now seen to have been, like the tabernacle in the wilderness, collapsible. In Christ God has come not only to pack it up, but to pack it away – permanently!

The result? Nothing that is distinctively Mosaic now stands between Jew and Gentile believers.

The Gentile believer is 'saved' (verse 8) through faith. The Jewish believer is 'saved' by faith. Both are saved by grace! There is no difference (*Gal.* 3:28; *Col.* 3:11)! The 'dividing wall of hostility' – a greater, longer-lasting barrier than the once infamous 'Berlin Wall' between East and West Germany – has been demolished. Christ *himself is our peace* and has *made us both one* (2:14).

We ought to re-read these words: *He himself is our peace*. They are emphatic. Not simply 'he is our peace' but he *himself*. Peace is not a commodity given to us by Christ; it is a reality experienced in fellowship with Christ. This echoes the emphasis with which the letter began: all blessings are ours fully, but only, in Christ.

We find the same emphasis in Jesus' Farewell Discourse (*John*. 13–17), when he described himself as the True Vine, his Father as the Vinedresser, and his disciples as branches (*John*. 15:1–11). The blessings of the gospel are not like grapes we can pick from a vine. No, they are more like the sap that flows through the branches that are part of the vine; we are the branches; Christ himself is the vine. We 'experience' the blessings only insofar as we are united to the vine in which the branches grow.

So here. We are at peace with God. Further, we are at peace with our fellow-believers whether Jew *(those who were near)* or Gentile (*who were far off*).

But there is more. We are not merely 'at peace'. *Christ himself is our peace* – and we enjoy and share *shalom* (peace in the fullest and richest biblical sense) only because we are united together in Christ who is our peace. Faith does not 'pick' blessings from Christ. Faith unites us to Christ, and thus united to him all spiritual blessings are ours, including being united to one another in him. This is *shalom*!

CHRIST PREACHES PEACE

Paul further elaborates how the message of the gospel has effected this. Christ, who is himself our peace, is also the One who preached that peace to us! Here is a preacher we can trust. He not only *practises* what he preaches; he *is* what he preaches!

Remember Luke's beautiful narrative of the climactic events of the first Easter Day. That evening, Jesus appeared to his confused disciples in Jerusalem. He – the One who was chastised to bring them peace (*Isa.* 53:5) – showed them his hands and feet. Jesus, crucified as a sacrifice for their sins, raised by the power of God for their salvation, was their peace! And the opening words of his Easter sermon to them? 'Peace to you' (*Luke.* 24:36). He who was their peace came to preach peace to them.

But Paul's words, however wonderfully they might describe the first Easter, actually refer to the experience of the Ephesians. When had Christ come to preach to them?

Christ lives for ever as Intercessor and is therefore our High Priest. He reigns until all his and our enemies become his footstool, and is our King. But he is also the true Prophet of God and as such he continues his ministry to and for his people. He continues to *preach peace.*

But how? He does so through the preaching of his word. As the Letter to the Hebrews expresses it, Christ continues to say: 'I will tell of your name to my brothers; in the midst of the congregation I will sing your praise' (*Heb.* 2:12). Interestingly, these words are cited from the triumph section of Psalm 22 and are understood by the author of Hebrews to refer to the resurrection ministry of the Messiah.

Similarly in Romans 10:14 Paul asks the question: 'How shall they believe in Him whom they have not heard?' (*New American Standard Bible*). True we cannot believe unless we have heard *about* Jesus. But Paul implies more than this. 'Him whom they have not heard' implies that in the proclamation of the gospel in the power of the Spirit we hear the living voice of Christ (see *John.* 10:3, 5, 16). Paul further implies that it is through the preachers the Lord has sent that he himself speaks.

We need to recover this New Testament teaching and learn to think of the preaching of the Word of God as an aspect of the ongoing work of Christ as Prophet. When hearts and minds are engaged by such preaching, there is a deep consciousness that Christ himself is speaking, indeed 'preaching' his Word to us. This, incidentally, is why preachers themselves must 'sit under the ministry of the Word' even while they are themselves preaching it so that they can be 'preached to' as really and powerfully as any of their hearers.

ALL HAVE ACCESS

We are one in Christ, because *through him we both [Jew and Gentile] have access in one Spirit to the Father* (2:18). Christ who is our Prophet and King is also the High Priest who gains access for us into the presence of the Father. And – just as is true of his ministry as King and Prophet – this privilege is extended to us through the ministry of the Holy Spirit. It takes nothing less than the concerted work of the three persons of the Trinity to bring us into fellowship with God.

The triune God has not been 'too proud' (so to speak) to grant us this privilege. Like Esther in the Old Testament, even when we are dressed in 'royal robes' we know we cannot approach the King on our own account, by our own authority. We must be granted *access* to him. The Great King holds out the golden sceptre of his grace to us in Christ. Esther-like we 'approach and touch the tip of the sceptre', and hear a voice from his throne of glory that says 'What is it . . . What is your request?' (*Esther* 5:1–3).

Too ashamed and reluctant to pray, to worship, to draw near to God, as we often are, the Father encourages us to come (he 'seeks' us, says Jesus, *John.* 4:23). He makes it possible for us to appear before him. For he has spared no expense in order to bring us every spiritual blessing. For this *access* is what Paul earlier meant when he said that we were *brought near* (2:13). It is made possible only *by the blood of Christ*.

Does this energize us to live in God's presence, to seek his face in worship, the ministry of his Word and prayer, and to enjoy the blessings of shared fellowship before him? He has given his Son for us (*Rom.* 8:32). Why should we be so slow to come to him, so reluctant to give everything we are and have to him? If he has given his Son for our brothers and sisters, how can we be ashamed of them, and at times even alienated from them? That contradicts the gospel Paul describes here.

If, then, we have 'access by faith into this grace in which we stand' (*Rom.* 5:2), let us stand in grace. In fact let us luxuriate in the blessings with which it surrounds us, and rejoice in sharing that grace without restriction with one another!

15

Fellow Citizens

So then you are no longer strangers and aliens, but you are fellow citizens with the saints and members of the household of God, [20]*built on the foundation of the apostles and prophets, Christ Jesus himself being the cornerstone,* [21]*in whom the whole structure, being joined together, grows into a holy temple in the Lord.* [22]*In him you also are being built together into a dwelling place for God by the Spirit.* (Eph. 2:19–22)

We are no longer what we once were. This is the conclusion Paul now reaches on the basis of his earlier teaching. We were *strangers* and *aliens*. Now we are *citizens* and *members of the household of God*. We belong in the kingdom of God, and we are children adopted into the family of God. We serve him as King and we love him as Father. We are the temple of God.

GOSPEL GRAMMAR

We have seen already that Paul's gospel (indeed *the* gospel) has a grammar all of its own. Misuse it and we distort the gospel and its grace. That basic grammar appears again here. It is on the basis of what Christ has done for us that there is a 'so then' – our privileges are the spiritual implications of what God, Father, Son, and Holy Spirit, has already accomplished for us. *This is the indicative-imperative rule*: what God has done grounds his summons to us to be faithful to him.

But there is another grammatical 'rule' to be learned, which Paul illustrates here. *No longer* (verse 19) is always accompanied by *but now* (cf. verse 13), whether or not the words themselves are actually used. If something that was true of our lives before we were 'in Christ' has been set aside, it is to be replaced by its opposite. This is the replacement rule: what we put off in life needs to give way to what we are to put on.

Once we grasp this rule of gospel grammar we will notice it in many different contexts in the New Testament. When specific sins are to be put away, they must be replaced by their antithetical graces (cf. *Rom.* 13:14; *Gal.* 5:16–24; *Eph.* 4:25; *Col.* 3:5–16). A gospel-centred life is built on the ground-plan created by the gospel itself: the death of the old cannot be separated from, but always leads to, the new resurrection life.

Paul works out this principle here too. We are *no longer strangers and aliens*. Positively, we have become *fellow citizens with the saints*; we belong to the *household of God* (verse 19)!

We are no longer what we once were. But Christian living involves more. We are now citizens in God's kingdom and members of his family. Formerly we were spiritually dead and in bondage to Satan, the world, and the flesh, by nature children of wrath, separated, strangers, aliens. Now our new identity both secures us (we belong!) and transforms us (we live as citizens and sons, no longer as aliens and orphans). In a world where people, young and old, have lost a sense of belonging and a direction in living, the gospel of Christ is good news indeed.

Paul draws our attention to three features of God's household: its home is built on a solid foundation; it grows constantly together into a temple; and it is built to be a dwelling place for the Holy Spirit.

SOLID FOUNDATIONS

The church is *built on the foundation of the apostles and prophets, Christ Jesus himself being the cornerstone* (2:20).

The *apostles and prophets* count for nothing apart from Jesus Christ. Their calling, gifts, and ministry all derive from the ascended Lord as Paul later says (4:7–12). Notice in passing here how the motifs, which Paul introduces, are sometimes developed later on in the letter. In other instances a whole passage will shed fresh light on something said earlier. This being the case Paul places great stress on the apostles' foundational role in the life of the church.

Three interesting, if slightly technical, questions arise here:

i. While Paul refers to apostles in the sense of 'The Twelve' and Paul (and perhaps some others), to whom does he refer when he speaks about 'prophets'? Are they the same people ('those individuals who are both apostles and prophets') or different ('those who are apostles and also those who are prophets')?

A single definite article ('the') covers both nouns here (*the apostles and prophets* not 'the apostles and the prophets'). That could indicate Paul is speaking about the same people (apostles who are prophets). On the other hand, in 4:11 he again mentions apostles and prophets in the same breath and in the same order, and in that context he clearly distinguishes between them. He is probably, therefore, thinking of two different groups here as well: the apostles appointed by the Lord (who, of course, were also prophets in their own right, bearers of divine revelation) and also others (who were) prophets in the churches.

ii. In what sense is it appropriate to speak of the church as *built on the foundation of the apostles and prophets* when elsewhere Paul says that Jesus Christ is the only foundation (*1 Cor.* 3:11)?

The genitive case here (the foundation *of* the apostles) may mean that they *laid* the foundation, *Christ Jesus himself,* rather than they themselves *being* the foundation. But the New Testament does teach that the apostles and prophets are part of the church's foundation. Jesus' promise to Simon Peter was that, in some sense, on him – with the other apostles – the church would be built. That happened on the Day of Pentecost through Peter's preaching. Jesus envisaged all later believers coming to faith through the testimony of the apostles (*John.* 17:20). The idea occurs again in John's vision of the New Jerusalem: 'the wall of the city had twelve foundations, and on them were the twelve names of the twelve apostles of the Lamb' (*Rev.* 21:14).

Christ gave his apostles the 'power of attorney' when he commissioned them (*Matt.* 28:18–20; *John.* 20:21–23). They did not share in his atoning work, but they were given a key role in his church-building vision.

This is what we mean when we speak about the '*apostolic* church'. We do not mean that an unbroken chain of the laying on of hands connects us all the way back to Simon Peter and then to Jesus himself. (Actually when Jesus commissioned the apostles, he 'showed them his hands' rather than 'laid on them' his hands! *John*. 20:20). The apostolic churches are those that confess Christ as Saviour and Lord, are faithful to apostolic teaching, serve him in the world, and look for his appearing and the consummation of his kingdom (cf. *1 Thess.* 1:9–10).

(iii) What role does Paul have in view when he speaks about Christ as the vital stone (ESV, *cornerstone*) in the building? The Greek word used can refer either to a 'cornerstone' – the key stone in the foundation – or a 'capstone' the crowning stone of the entire building. The first well expresses the idea of Christ as foundation; the second fits well with the idea that the building is built up into Christ.

The background to what Paul is saying is probably to be found in the words of Isaiah 28:16 (cited in various contexts in the New Testament, *Rom.* 9:33; *1 Pet.* 2:6): 'Behold, I am the one who has laid as a foundation in Zion, a stone, a tested stone, a precious cornerstone, of a sure foundation.' The whole church is viewed here as being built on, held together in place by, taking its fundamental shape from, Jesus the cornerstone. He is the stone on which all else depends.

GROWING INTO A TEMPLE

Paul now takes the building metaphor one step further; it is no ordinary house God is constructing, but *a holy temple* (verse 21). But this temple is built on Christ and is one in which all believers (whether Jew or Gentile) share in the blessings promised to God's covenant people.

The privileges of the old covenant pointed forward to the rich spiritual privileges that would be realized in Christ. Now, Paul adds, this extends to the very heart of Old Testament religion – to the temple itself. God is now building a new covenant temple; not a physical one in Jerusalem, but an international temple constructed of living stones. The Christian temple is built of Christians!

Think of what this must have meant to believers who lived their whole lives under the shadow of the Temple of Diana! Dwarfed – both physically and spiritually – as they sometimes must have felt – they needed to learn to walk not by sight but by faith. *They* were God's true temple. Indeed, in the next chapter Paul will add that they – not the Diana Temple – were the true 'wonder of the world'. In them the universe of powers would see the handiwork of divine wisdom and be in awe (3:10)!

BUILT TOGETHER

Paul has spoken about the new temple structure being *joined together* (verse 21) and now speaks of the Ephesians being *built together* to be *a dwelling place for God by the Spirit*. The double emphasis here (joined *together*, built *together*) reminds us that the church is not an aggregate of diverse people, but individuals united to each other in their union with Jesus Christ. They are brought closer to one another in Christ, united together like the great stones of the Jerusalem temple. The stones were so perfectly carved by the skilled stonemasons that they fitted perfectly, sustained one another in place, and took the weight of the next level of building. What a marvellous picture of the church!

Imagine those temple stones had voices as the masons worked on them, as the haulage teams moved them into place, as master craftsmen shaped them to fit perfectly with each other! What cries of pain, what refusal of design, what complaint about the shape, or size of neighbouring stones might we hear! So it is in the church. Christ builds from living stones, sinners who are resistant material, difficult to shape, reluctant to fit with other living stones. Yet Christ continues to build – for he means to come himself, by his Spirit, to dwell among us as his house and temple (*1 Cor*. 3:16–17). He wants to be able to point to the church in the world and say: 'See, that is what I can do. See my wisdom, power and love' (cf. 3:10)!

One day the scaffolding will be taken away and the entire cosmos will see the First Wonder of the New World!

16

Prisoner of Christ, Steward of the Mystery

For this reason I, Paul, a prisoner for Christ Jesus on behalf of you Gentiles –[2]*assuming that you have heard of the stewardship of God's grace that was given to me for you,* [3]*how the mystery was made known to me by revelation, as I have written briefly.* [4]*When you read this, you can perceive my insight into the mystery of Christ,* [5]*which was not made known to the sons of men in other generations as it has now been revealed to his holy apostles and prophets by the Spirit.* [6]*This mystery is that the Gentiles are fellow heirs, members of the same body, and partakers of the promise in Christ Jesus through the gospel.* (Eph. 3:1–6)

In the first forty-five verses of Ephesians there is only one verb in the imperative (commanding) mood. And that was an exhortation not so much to do something new but to remember what we once were.

Now, as Paul continues, he is transitioning to a series of exhortations: *For this reason I, Paul, a prisoner* . . . to break off his train of thought and return to it only later: *I therefore, a prisoner . . . urge you to* . . . (4:1).

Paul is about to urge the Ephesians to respond to the grace of God in an appropriate manner. He has the authority to do this not only as an apostle (1:1), but because he is *a prisoner for Christ Jesus on behalf of . . . Gentiles* (cf. 4:1).

As these words come from Paul's lips their significance dawns on him all over again: Saul of Tarsus, rabid persecutor of the infant church, the man whose hands were tainted with the blood of martyrs, Pharisee of Pharisees – but now (i) in prison *for Christ Jesus*? and (ii) a prisoner *for the sake of Gentiles*? Amazing!

Note Paul's self-description! He is *a prisoner for Christ Jesus*, willing to suffer for him. Moreover, he is also devoted to the evangelism of *the Gentiles*.

These words take us back to his Damascus Road experience and its aftermath (e.g. *Acts* 9:15, 16). From the beginning he was appointed as a prophet to the nations and to suffering for the gospel. He shows no self-pity ('If only I could have been sent to others and could have avoided suffering!'). Rather he has embraced God's calling.

Paul knew who he was, and knew what he was *for*. That was a liberating reality for him, focusing his mind, enabling him to prioritise. In a time of personal deprivation he knew God had a purpose where others thought his life seemed bleak. As he wrote to the Philippians, what had happened to him had really turned out to advance the gospel (*Phil.* 1:12). As he comments later in this chapter, his sufferings should not create loss of heart for any of his friends but instead are their glory (verse 13)!

AN UNKNOWN AUTHOR

What follows seems a curious qualification: *assuming that you have heard of the stewardship of God's grace that was given to me for you* (3:2). Why 'assuming . . . '? Had any of them not heard? How could that be when he had been in Ephesus over an extended period of time (*Acts* 19:10)? Did the recipients of this letter *not* know Paul?

Some scholars point to these words as one indication that Ephesians could not have been written by Paul. But in fact – as often is the case – the explanation for them may lie in a commonplace pastoral experience. In a cosmopolitan church setting it is amazing how much the congregation may change within a short space of time. Someone who served as pastor only a few years ago may well be a total stranger to more recent members. Moreover, even the present pastor will be wise not to assume that every member has a firm grasp of what he has been teaching!

In addition, as we have noted, this letter may have been written for a broader readership than the church in Ephesus. There are quite natural reasons, therefore, for Paul to have written as he did. Such was his relationship to these churches that it was appropriate for him to 'assume' that those who had never met him would nevertheless know about him.

STEWARD OF THE GOSPEL

What, however, was Paul assuming? That they knew why he was *a prisoner for Christ* (not, notice, of Rome!) specifically *on behalf of you Gentiles*. Even although his first entrée into a city was at the door of the local synagogue if one existed, his special *stewardship* of the gospel was to bring it to *Gentiles*.

Paul – apostle (1:1), intercessor (1:15–16) – is also Paul the steward (cf. *1 Cor*. 4:1). He receives supplies from the Master of the house; his task is to dispense them to the household (2:19). He is a man under authority, accountable to his Master. It is an apt picture of Paul, and it is not surprising that he uses it for other ministers of the gospel (*Tit*. 1:7; cf. *1 Tim*. 3:4). Their task is not to be inventors, but stewards.

This stewardship is further described as *of God's grace* (cf. 3:7, 8). Again and again the apostle strikes this note – the gospel is a message of grace. This is what he has been exemplifying in the first two chapters of the letter, as well as in the last quarter century of his life.

THE MYSTERY REVEALED

Mystery in the New Testament, as we have already noticed, does not mean something 'spooky', but something that is hidden and to which we would have no access without divine revelation.

In verses 3–6 Paul takes us through several stages in redemptive history to underline the privilege he, the Ephesians, and we, share in the light of the coming of Christ:

- The mystery was *hidden for ages in God* (3:9).
- The mystery was *not made known to the sons of men in other generations* in the way it has now been revealed (3:5).
- The mystery *has now been revealed to [God's] holy apostles and prophets by the Spirit* (3:5).

- The mystery was *made known to [Paul] by revelation* (3:3).

Paul is astonished that he, of all people, fits into this flow of God's redemptive purposes. He sees further stages even in his own relationship to the mystery: revelation, illumination, proclamation, inscripturation.

1. He received *revelation.*

Presumably he is here reflecting on his experience on the Damascus Road and thereafter.

2. He experienced further *illumination* into the revelation.
   It was the basis for the increasing understanding of its meaning (or better of the meaning of Jesus Christ) given to him by the Spirit (3:4). In Paul's case both the original revelation and the ongoing illumination constituted the fullness of the revelation of Christ. His *insight into the mystery of Christ* was a special work of God. His gospel is not a human creation (cf. Gal. 1:12).
3. He communicated this insight in *proclamation.*
   In doing so Paul passed on the *revelation* in his gospel teaching. That is implied in 3:2. But he now takes this one stage further:
4. He preserved and propagated all this by *inscripturation.*
   He has already written *briefly* about it (3:3; probably a reference back to 1:7–10); now it should be even clearer when the Ephesians read on.

It is sometimes suggested that Paul would have been staggered to discover people like ourselves studying his letters two thousand years after they were first written. This suggestion usually implies the idea that Paul did not regard his letters as the church has done since his time – authoritative, divinely inspired documents – a canon.

In fact, there are signs in Paul's letters that he well realized the profound significance of his role as an apostle. He was a chosen instrument to give the revelation of Christ to the world. His letters, like the torah in the synagogue, were to be 'read' in the churches (cf. 3:4). Paul knew that his letters were to carry the authority of God among his people in the same way the Scriptures of the Old Testament did. Further evidence for this lies in the fact that already when Second Peter was being written a collection of his letters was already being treated on a par with other Scripture, and was being interpreted – falsely – in the churches (see *2 Pet.* 3:15–16).

But this leaves us still with the central question: What is this mystery revealed to Paul? He has already given us the basic answer in 1:9–10. Now he enlarges on it:

Believing *Gentiles* now receive all the blessings of God.
Believing *Gentiles* are among the elect!
Believing *Gentiles* are now brothers and sisters with believing Jews.
Believing *Gentiles* now inherit the promises of God!
Gentiles are*: Fellow heirs, members of the same body, and partakers of the promise* (3:6).

Praise God that every Christian believer, from every tribe, tongue, people, and nation, is 'in on' the secret! What was hidden in God's eternal plan, but only in veiled ways understood by the prophets, has now been realized in Jesus Christ and revealed to us through the apostolic preaching in the Scriptures – is a secret to us no more!

This mystery is not 'Plan B'. It is the eternal plan. It is, therefore, 'Plan A'. There is no 'Plan B'. And now the secret is out – for everyone who knows Christ.

17

Unsearchable Riches

Of this gospel I was made a minister according to the gift of God's grace, which was given me by the working of his power. [8]*To me, though I am the very least of all the saints, this grace was given, to preach to the Gentiles the unsearchable riches of Christ,* [9]*and to bring to light for everyone what is the plan of the mystery hidden for ages in God who created all things* (Eph. 3:7–9).

Paul did not think of himself as a prisoner of the Emperor, although he was in Roman custody. He was a prisoner 'for Christ Jesus', because of his passionate desire to fulfil his commission to bring the gospel to the Gentiles. He well illustrates an important spiritual principle. What we make of the situations in which we find ourselves depends largely on our perspective, or more exactly, on how Christ-centred our thinking is.

THE NATURE OF GOSPEL MINISTRY

Already, Paul has spoken about his service as a 'stewardship of God's grace' (3:2). Now he speaks of being a *minister* of the gospel (3:7). Marvellously and almost unconsciously he underlines that the common factor between the two ideas is *grace* (verses 2, 7). As steward of grace he is himself dependent on that grace in order to minister the grace of the gospel. So the gospel and its ministry flow from grace and point to grace. It is grace from start to finish, from first to last – all 'to the praise of his glorious grace' (1:6).

There is a special lesson here for ministers and pastors, but it is applicable to every Christian. In whatever form of service we engage we live out of the very same resources to which we point others.

Indeed, the gifts that enable us to do this are themselves expressions of the grace they communicate. Paul was *a minister according to the gift of God's grace* (3:7). Gifts for ministry do not raise us 'above' those to whom we minister. Rather they are the grace-and-favour-gifts of Christ to enable the otherwise handicapped and paralysed to express God's love to others.

Paul was deeply conscious of this in his own life and ministry. He describes himself as *the very least of all the saints* (verse 8) or more literally, 'the lesser least of all saints'. His self-description defies the ordinary rules of grammar: he uses a comparative ('lesser') of a superlative ('least'). One cannot be less than the least! But Paul sees himself, as it were, at the bottom of the pile. There is, surely, a close relationship between that disposition, produced by God's grace, Paul's desire to see others receive that grace, and the grace-inspired energy with which he laboured so fruitfully.

The servants of Christ live in a never-ending cycle, in which, conscious of our sin and weakness we depend on the grace of Christ. In that dependence we begin to see ourselves as servants rather than masters of our fellow-believers. Thus we kneel before them (*2 Cor.* 4:5b). With a servant spirit (Jesus-like!) and enabled by the gifts of his grace (whether preaching, organizing, shepherding, caring, or helping) we say 'The Lord Jesus loves you, and he has given me this gift to help me to express his love for you and to add my own.' I must learn to use my spiritual gifts as if I were writing a love letter to the one to whom I seek to minister.

THE GOAL OF PAUL'S MINISTRY

In various places Paul indicates the motivations and goals which drove him on in the face of persecution, discouragement, suffering and many other burdens (e.g. *2 Cor.* 4:1ff.). In the last analysis these were all concentrated in the one great motive that served as the refrain of his opening doxology: the praise of the glory of God, and the honour of his grace. But the engine that drove him towards God's glory had many different parts, all working together in subsidiary ways to produce the enormous energy of his ministry.

Paul was called to glorify God through the proclamation of the gospel to the Gentiles. This was his specific grace-gift (*To me . . .*

this grace was given, to preach to the Gentiles the unsearchable riches of Christ, verse 8).

The words are remarkable in their own right, for reasons Paul later enumerated to Timothy (*1 Tim.* 1:12–17). They virtually defined his own Christian life. In his case conversion to Christ and his calling to service to the Gentiles were two sides of the same coin – a fact that astonished his new friend Ananias almost as much as it did Saul of Tarsus himself (*Acts* 9:10–16).

This pattern in which the context and experience of calling and the specific burden of an individual are integrally related is not unusual. Think, for example of Isaiah (*Isa.* 6:1ff.) and Jeremiah (*Jer.* 1:1ff.). The burden of their ministries was an expression of the way in which God had called them to serve him. It is often this way and was so for Saul of Tarsus.

UNSEARCHABLE RICHES

Paradoxically what Paul was called to preach to the Gentiles was the *riches of Christ*. The riches of the Messiah – *for the Gentiles*! The very idea was staggering. In addition those riches are *unsearchable* (3:8. The same term is used in *Rom.* 11:33 of God's ways). The word means 'without footprint'. We see the love of Christ revealed in his words and acts, supremely in the cross. But as we trace that love back to its source in God the Trinity we realize its footprints lead us back to what Paul elsewhere calls 'the depths of God' (*1 Cor.* 2:10).

Nor is this the only paradox. As Paul preaches he brings out into the open *the mystery*, which *for ages* had been known only within the eternal fellowship of God the Trinity. No wonder he had an overwhelming sense of the grace of God – that he, of all people, should have this task and privilege. Who in the world would have chosen Saul of Tarsus, rabid hater of Christians, and persecutor of the church to accomplish this? Who, but God, would set his heart on 'the foremost' of 'sinners' (*1 Tim.* 1:15) to make him the chief divine instrument to break out of Judaism to bring the gospel of Christ to the Gentiles?

Only God could devise such a scheme. And yet there is a deep appropriateness about it. God is the One who has already overturned all human expectations by taking our flesh. He has shown his wisdom in the foolishness of the cross, and his power in the weakness of his Son's death, who uses foolish things to confound the wise (*1 Cor.* 1:27–29). How amazing to take a hater of the Gentiles to be the vehicle of Christ's love for them. Yes, it is paradoxical – *yet how like God*!

Two statements here run parallel to each another: Paul was called to a ministry of:

Preaching the unsearchable riches of Christ

and

Bringing to light the plan of the mystery hidden for ages in God.

PREACHING THE WORD

Paul was a recipient and communicator of new revelation in a way we are not. Yet the ministry of the gospel today involves the same revelation. In this sense, the calling of those who preach is to *bring to light* the mystery of the gospel. The verb means 'to light up'. This is the goal of the preaching of the Word of God in the power of the Spirit of God – light (not just heat!)!

As Paul puts it in 1 Corinthians 4:2, 5–6, in true preaching a threefold illumination takes place:

(i) of the truth of the gospel to the mind of the individual
(ii) of the integrity of the preacher to the conscience of the listener
(iii) of the life of the hearer to his or her need of grace.

As a steward of the gospel, Paul was always going to the 'cupboards' stocked with its truth, and bringing out into the light the provisions of his Master. Yes, it is good when biblical exposition is full of heat. But God's Son never gives out heat without at the same time giving light. These, then, are the hallmarks and watchwords of true preaching in the Pauline tradition: light, illumination, clarification, manifestation, and understanding. They should be the hallmarks of all preaching.

From all eternity an exclusive secret has been shared by the three persons of the Godhead. How and when angels and archangels, cherubim and seraphim, came to learn about it we do not know. We know that its unfolding was of intense interest and concern to them as well as to the Old Testament prophets (*1 Pet.* 1:10–12). No wonder, since it concerned their King and Master!

But now this secret has been revealed to us – to us whose salvation from sin and death and Satan required nothing less than the death of God the Son in our flesh. Neither Old Testament prophets nor wise men, neither archangels nor seraphim, possessed the plumb line to sound the depths of such a plan of divine grace. But we know. We have been told. We have been enlightened.

There is no creature in heaven or earth more privileged than the humblest believer who has come to understand the depth of this great mystery!

18

Multi-Coloured Wisdom

To me, though I am the very least of all the saints, this grace was given, to preach to the Gentiles the unsearchable riches of Christ, [9]and to bring to light for everyone what is the plan of the mystery hidden for ages in God who created all things, [10]so that through the church the manifold wisdom of God might now be made known to the rulers and authorities in the heavenly places. [11]This was according to the eternal purpose that he has realized in Christ Jesus our Lord, [12]in whom we have boldness and access with confidence through our faith in him. [13]So I ask you not to lose heart over what I am suffering for you, which is your glory. (Eph. 3:8–13)

Paul seems to have been an expert at 'multi-tasking'. In fact, however, he was always pursuing a few central goals – indeed ultimately one central goal: to know, love, and serve Christ and to glorify God (cf. *Phil.* 3:13b). This was what gave him energy to build the church of Christ (*Col.* 1:29). Although he was intensely interested in individuals – like Onesimus the runaway slave (*Philem.* 10) – his vision was not individualistic but corporate. He did not seek to win individual converts merely, but to plant churches wherever he went.

Paul saw very clearly that the church has a central role in the purpose of God. Here he expresses that purpose in a way that illustrates his calling – to preach in such a way that he brought to light, for those with faith to see, the divine plan of the ages.

THE CHURCH – THE THEATRE OF GOD'S WISDOM

The initial impact of Paul's preaching was to bring people into God's kingdom here in the world. But now he takes a wide view of what God is doing. The result of the gospel is the creation of a new community (*the church*). God is creating this fellowship, and building it on solid foundations (cf. 2:20), as living proof of his *wisdom* (verse 10). It is the sphere in which he makes that wisdom known to the heavenly powers.

This stunning statement raises several questions. What is this *manifold wisdom* and how is it made known *through the church*? Who are *the rulers and authorities in the heavenly places* to whom it is made known?

The *wisdom of God* – his ability to reach his own goals in ways that are best and most consistent with his character – is present in everything he does (cf. *Prov.* 8). But here Paul has in mind the special wisdom displayed in the existence and life of the church.

This is the wisdom seen in the incarnation and crucifixion – what seems folly and weakness but in fact is the design of God to bring salvation to sinners. Its fruit appears in the church. It is seen also in the rich diversity of people the Lord fits together into the church. He is creating a new kind of international community, a people who experience the power of Christ's resurrection. There is nothing remotely like this to be seen anywhere else in the universe. Those who are in Christ, and thus belong to his church, together display the wisdom of the plan of salvation.

The word here translated *manifold* was sometimes used in secular Greek to mean 'multi-coloured'. It expresses the rich diversity and variety of forms in which God's wisdom comes to expression in the community that belongs to Christ. God is an artist who paints in many different hues. One obvious example was the Jew-Gentile reconciliation, fellowship, and mutual devotion that the gospel created. But the principle is applicable to many aspects of the church.

The *principalities and powers* Paul has in view are spectators of God's wisdom. Later in the letter he uses a very similar expression to describe the powers of darkness (*Eph.* 6:12). Perhaps Paul is thinking that the very existence of the church and the restoration of true community life in it is a sign to the sinister network of spiritual evil that God has fulfilled the promise of Genesis 3:1. The head of the serpent has been bruised; the gates of Hades cannot prevail against the church building programme of the Lord Jesus (*Matt.* 16:18–20)!

Of course, holy angels are also spectators of the church, and as Peter hints, are keenly interested in the wonder of our salvation (*1 Pet.* 1:12). They are, after all, part of the same family which spans heaven and earth. They delight to explore the *eternal purpose . . . realized in Christ Jesus our Lord* (3:11). It is possible that Paul has them particularly in mind.

ON NOT LOSING HEART

Now we understand why Paul adds that in Christ *we have boldness and access with confidence through our faith* (verse 12). *Boldness*, *access*, *confidence*, *faith* – these words ring with a sense of God's triumphant purposes being fulfilled. The gospel lifts our spirits. That is why Paul encourages the Ephesians *not to lose heart over what I am suffering for you* (verse 13).

Our native instinct when 'bad things' happen is *to lose heart*. This verb appears in secular Greek to describe the experience of a woman giving birth – finding the strain so great that she feels she cannot sustain the hours of child labour. So in the stresses and strains of serving Christ the pressures may overwhelm us.

In this particular instance the discouraging thing was that the voice of Paul – of all people – had apparently been silenced. This was no 'ordinary' Christian. Surely it was a disaster? The Ephesians needed Paul. All the churches needed him. The very cause of the gospel itself needed him. If this kind of thing happened to Paul, what hope was there?

SUFFERING AND GLORY

But Paul had a very different view of reality! Notice what he says about his suffering:

It is for the Ephesians. He had already stated this in general in 3:1 – he was a prisoner for the sake of the Gentiles. Now he makes it more specific. His imprisonment was an expression of the lengths to which he was prepared to go for their salvation – and that in turn was an expression of the length to which Christ had already gone for them.

It creates glory. The apostle sees an integral relationship between his suffering and the 'glory' of the Ephesians. How can *his* suffering be *their* glory?

Suffering and glory go hand in hand for Paul (cf. *Rom*. 8:18; *2 Cor*. 4:17). The relationship is never simply chronological (suffering *now*, glory *then*); it is causal – glory *because of* suffering. Indeed for Paul suffering is the raw material out of which glory is created.

Here he underlines that this is not simply a connection in the individual (my suffering will lead to my glory). We can understand that, as God works in us through affliction, it can be used to cleanse and transform us, to humble us, to make us gentle and more sympathetic towards others. But here Paul claims that his suffering has the Ephesians' glory in view – indeed, it *is* their glory!

This amazing statement is by no means an isolated thought for Paul. Certainly the glory of the Ephesians lies in how much he is prepared to suffer for them. He loves them that much. But more is in view. Paul's suffering for them has their glorification in view. He speaks about 'death' working in him so that 'life' may work in others (*2 Cor*. 4:12). He endures everything – opposition of all kinds, suffering in different dimensions – for the sake of the elect – 'that they also may obtain the salvation that is in Christ Jesus with eternal glory' (*2 Tim*. 2:10; see also the profound words in *Col*. 1:24 in which Paul speaks about his share in the afflictions of Christ).

The suffering of Jesus led to his glory; but it also leads to our glorification. All suffering that is experienced 'in Christ' as part of our union and communion with him, makes us like a grain of wheat that falls into the soil and dies – in order to bear much fruit (cf. *John*. 12:24). The life that refuses to sacrifice for others (the seed that refuses to 'die') will remain alone, in solitude, unconnected to the fellowship of God's people. The person who refuses to be shaped by the Builder of the temple bears little lasting fruit.

Gifts alone do not bear fruit for Christ. They have to be set within the pattern established by Christ. His fullness of the gifts of the Spirit (*John*. 3:34) was set within the context of suffering which would lead to glory. The way of the Master settled for Paul the way of the servant.

Who but the all-wise God would have thought of producing glory out of suffering? Again and again in Paul's writings this theme emerges: the pattern the Father used in the ministry of his Son is . . . *the* pattern.

The wisdom of God, then, is displayed in the church, first in Christ its foundation, then in Paul as its wise master-builder, and now in all believers as they serve together.

This wisdom is indeed multi-coloured! But do we have the wisdom to see the pattern of its working in our lives? This, too, is part of understanding the mystery which has been made known in Christ.

19

Bending the Knee

For this reason I bow my knees before the Father, [15]from whom every family in heaven and on earth is named, [16]that according to the riches of his glory he may grant you to be strengthened with power through his Spirit in your inner being, [17]so that Christ may dwell in your hearts through faith – that you, being rooted and grounded in love, [18]may have strength to comprehend with all the saints what is the breadth and length and height and depth, [19]and to know the love of Christ that surpasses knowledge, that you may be filled with all the fullness of God. (Eph. 3:14–19)

At the beginning of this chapter it seemed that Paul had gone off at a tangent from his central theme. If so, it was a thrilling tangent! It is likely that he does not pick up the thread of his earlier thoughts until chapter four. Although he here repeats the words with which the chapter opened – *for this reason* (verse 1, verse 14) – the *reason* for the prayer that follows is to be found in verses 1–13. God has broken the neck of the dark powers; he has raised the spiritually dead to new life; he has brought reconciliation in Christ – and he has subdued Saul of Tarsus and called him to be the apostle to the Gentiles.

Paul's instinct in the face of such marvellous wisdom is – to kneel (*ESV*, more literally, *I bow my knees*). The words echo Isaiah 45:23: 'To me every knee shall bow, every tongue shall swear allegiance' (words re-echoed in *Phil.* 2:10; and *Rom.* 14:11). This is not grandiose speech; it is the worship that is due to the exalted Lord. Paul does not wait for the final day when this will take place; he wishes to honour the Lord now.

The Old Testament background to these words is significant for a further reason. The New Testament authors were conscious of the context of the Old Testament texts they cited. Given their Jewish education they had probably memorized much of the Old Testament and knew it by heart. So Paul knew that Isaiah's words were prefaced by an invitation to 'all the ends of the earth' to turn to the Lord and be saved. This is exactly what he saw taking place in his own lifetime, through his own ministry (*Rom.* 15:8–21)! His kneeling is not a formal religious habit, but the deep instinct of someone who senses that the only appropriate position before this great God is to lower oneself before him in admiration and awe.

THE FATHER

Paul bows *before the Father* in prayer. Characteristically, although not exclusively, prayer in the New Testament is addressed to the Father. He is described here as the One *from whom every [or the whole] family in heaven and earth is named.*

The same Greek word can be rendered either 'every' or 'all'. Thus Paul refers either to

- The fact that every *family* (grouping) in heaven and earth has its origin (*is named*) and should have its reference point in the Fatherhood of God,

  or

- The way the whole family in heaven and earth belongs to him, and bears the 'family name'.

Both possibilities stress the unity of the family of God. But Paul may be thinking about the way the one family of God is made up of different 'clans' – perhaps thinking of the 'clan' of angels and the 'clan' of redeemed believers in heaven, as well as the 'clan' of believers on earth, and, for all we know, 'clans' of cherubim and seraphim, and other non-human creatures of God who live in his presence.

Here is a further reason to kneel. Christians belong to this world-wide, history-long, heaven-and-earth family all sharing one and the same God and Father!

These words must have brought further strong encouragement to Paul's original readers and hearers, surrounded as they were by 'rulers . . . authorities . . . cosmic powers . . . this present darkness' (6:12). Christians also belong to a vast community – but under the fatherly care of God! And Paul can pray that the Ephesians will be *strengthened with power*, since the One to whom he prays is 'God the Father Almighty, Maker of heaven and earth'.

Here, as elsewhere, the apostle lingers lovingly on such thoughts. God will meet his friends' needs from his *riches in glory*. He will do so by a divine agent: *his Spirit*; the strengthening will reach their deepest needs: *in your inner being*.

But why would we need *to be strengthened*? Because our hearts are too weak and narrow to contain the treasure that God places in them: *that Christ may dwell in your hearts through faith*. His presence, as the Lord of all, is too weighty, too intensely holy and too grand for any of us to bear. If we are amazed that the manger in the stable could have held the Lord of all creation, it should be even more amazing to us that Christ himself comes to dwell in us. Yet he does.

CHRIST INDWELLING – THE BLESSING

The burden of Paul's prayer here is all too rare. Do we really believe that we need to *be strengthened with power through his Spirit in [y]our inner being, so that Christ may dwell in [y]our hearts through faith*?

Fail to see this and we reveal how little we understand or appreciate the magnitude of what God has done in us. His Son, the Creator whom the heaven of heavens cannot contain, the mighty Lord described earlier (1:21–22), comes to *dwell* in frail and sinful mortals! (The verb *dwell* here usually means to 'take up permanent residence', not merely 'to stay for a while'.) The magnitude of this is too much for us to take in fully. But when we begin to appreciate it and live in its light, the effect is life changing. This is why Paul had earlier prayed that the Ephesians would be able to grasp it (1:18) and why he now prays that we may be inwardly strengthened to be fit for it.

KNOWING CHRIST'S LOVE – THE EFFECT

Paul now enlarges on the result of the empowering of the Spirit and the indwelling of Christ. It is that, anchored (*rooted and grounded*) in love the Ephesians may further be able to appreciate the vastness of the love of Christ.

The language here is drawn from the worlds of horticulture and architecture. Love – the love of God in Christ – is the soil in which Christians thrive. It is also the foundation by which they will be shaped as their life of faith is built. The Ephesians need to know the dimensions of that love.

Paul speaks about being able *to comprehend* and *to know* this love in its *breadth and length and height and depth* (3:18) – although it *surpasses knowledge*. These are familiar words. We may scarcely give them a second thought. But they have two unusual features:

(i) We usually measure spatial objects in three dimensions – breadth, length and *either* height *or* depth – not four (height *and* depth being identical).

Some scholars have suggested that Paul's wording may reflect the language of the occult arts widely practised in Ephesus, in which some of these converts had once been engaged. They had celebrated their new life by a public 'book burning' (*Acts* 19:18–19). But perhaps they needed ongoing assurance that every dimension of the evil that once held them captive – its breadth, length, depth, and height – had met its match in the multi-dimensional character of the love of Christ.

Or it may simply be that the apostle's mind is here reflecting on the fact that the love of Christ needs to be seen not only in terms of its length and breadth, reaching out to the four corners of the earth, but that to measure its size involves contemplating the depths to which the Son of God stooped (cf. *Phil.* 2:5–8) and the height to which he has been exalted to the right hand of the Father (*Phil.* 2:9–11; *Rom.* 8:34).

(ii) Paul prays that the Ephesians will *comprehend . . . and . . . know the love of Christ that surpasses knowledge* (verses 18–19). This is a marvellous paradox on which to meditate – comprehending the incomprehensible, knowing what surpasses knowledge! Truly

> 'the love of Jesus, what it is,
> none but his loved ones know'.[1]

[1] From the hymn 'Jesus the very thought of thee', based on the words of Bernard of Clairvaux, translated by Edward Caswall.

TOGETHER

Paul prays that the Ephesians will comprehend Christ's love *with all the saints* (3:18). We are not isolated individuals, but 'fellow citizens' and belong to one family (2:19). Christ's love is not for us only, but for all who are his.

We need each other in order to grasp the measure of Christ's love as he makes it visible in the lives of our fellow-believers. We need to be taught and encouraged by them in order to understand it better. We need to receive from them the fruit of the grace-gifts that Christ has given to them in order to bring a sense of his love to us.

Nor should we limit this to our own church fellowship, or even to the contemporary church. Since it will take all of the saints in every age to express the fullness of Christ's love – to that extent I need every other Christian who has ever lived or shall ever live!

FILLED FULL

The end result of this is that we *may be filled with all the fullness of God* (3:19). The concept of fullness is a recurring one in Ephesians. Already we have learned that the church is 'the fullness of him who fills all in all' (1:23). Later Paul will speak about the church growing to the stature of the 'fullness of Christ'. Here he is praying that God's fullness will fill us – not so that we may be deified, but that we may so be indwelt by the Lord that we will be 'filled to capacity' as it were with the Lord's Spirit and therefore with his love.

This, then, is the fruit of Paul's prayer that we may *know the love of Christ*. But what does it mean to know Christ's love? It means to know that he loves me. How do I know what kind of love that is – what its *breadth, length, height, and depth* are?

Paul had already given the answer in an earlier letter: 'The Son of God . . . loved me and gave himself [on the cross] for me' (*Gal.* 2:20). He gave it again in what is usually regarded as his greatest letter: 'God shows his love for us in that while we were still sinners, Christ died for us' (*Rom.* 5:8). There – at the cross – is where we learn how great his love for us really is. Thanks be to God!

Should we ourselves not take time to bow the knee now?

20

To God Be the Glory

Now to him who is able to do far more abundantly than all that we ask or think, according to the power at work within us, [21]to him be glory in the church and in Christ Jesus throughout all generations, for ever and ever. Amen. (Eph. 3:20–21)

Our studies have brought us almost to the end of part one of Paul's magnificent letter. In that connection all kinds of interesting questions arise. Did he draft an outline before the letter was written? Did he ever revise? Sometimes it is assumed that divine inspiration meant that parts (if not all!) of Paul's letters poured out of his lips at breakneck speed. The grand sentence of Ephesians 1:3–14, for example, reads as though it were uttered in one breath! But we know enough about ancient letter writing, and the poor materials used in the first century, to understand that fast writing was virtually impossible. Inspiration is not a matter of ecstatic speech. Presumably there were frequent pauses as Paul dictated.

In any event, the words at the end of Ephesians 3 mark a pause as Paul transitions from exposition to application. As we have seen, the sole imperative in Ephesians 1–3 exhorts the readers to remember what they once were. Ephesians chapters 4–6 by contrast contain, in one form or another, dozens of imperatives.

But before we turn to Paul's exhortations we also need to take deep breaths of grace to enable us to take in and apply all that will follow.

STRETCHING TO THE LIMIT

Paul has been stretching his intercessory petitions to the limit. He dared to ask that the Ephesians would know that Christ's love for them is more expansive than the strength of the evil powers that formerly held them in bondage (2:2–3). He had also prayed that they would 'be filled with all the fullness of God' (3:19).

Now, however, he has even more to say. Our prayers cannot stretch to the limits of what God is able to do. For that reason Paul's intercession in 3:14–19 gives way to adoration and doxology. It is as if, having uttered the majestic earlier words, he himself reflects on them. But rather than revise them as though he had exaggerated, he realizes that he needs to extend them further. For God is *able to do far more abundantly than all that we ask or think!*

This statement should be savoured, its taste lingering in our mouths long after we have read it, because it represents a build up of thought that breaks through the limits of language. Paul's words make genuine contact with the truth he wants to express. Yet at the same time they point to a reality he cannot express in words. This is perhaps best expressed if we think of an ascending series of ideas:

God can do

- All we ask
- All we ask or think of asking
- More than all we can ask or think of asking
- More abundantly than all we can ask or think
- Far more abundantly than all we can ask or think

Ordinarily adjectives and adverbs have a comparative ('more') and a superlative ('most') form. Here Paul uses what has been called a 'super-superlative'. Our ability to ask, indeed our ability to conceive what we might ask, cannot stretch to the limits of what God can actually accomplish. Nor is this merely an abstract or theoretical idea. Rather it is *according to the power at work within us.*

Paul has been at pains to point out that, while transcendent, God is not remote from us; he has come, in the Spirit of his Son, to indwell us, so that we might be filled with his fullness (3:19). This is in fact the fullness of the One who fills all things. This fulfils the promise Jesus himself made that the Father and the Son would come to make their dwelling in believers, through the coming of the Spirit (*John.* 14:21, 23).

No wonder Paul sings *to him be glory*! Nor are these words a vague expression of upbeat emotion. In the phrases that follow he makes explicit where the glory of God is to be seen.

GOD'S GLORY IN THE CHURCH

For Paul the *glory* of God was almost a physical reality. From time to time throughout the history of redemption God had revealed it in powerful ways that his people could see and at times almost touch, taste, and smell (cf. e.g. *Isa.* 6:1ff.). His glory is the visible expression of his invisible perfection, a display of the harmony of all of his personal characteristics.

Paul had already hinted at one of the ways in which God displays aspects of his character when he spoke about the church as the sphere in which his wisdom can be observed (3:10). Now he is praying that the church will be the sphere in which God's glory as a whole will be put on display. The church, as Peter notes, is called 'to proclaim the excellencies [perfections, virtues] of him who called you out of darkness into his marvellous light' (*1 Pet.* 2:9).

This is a wide-reaching principle with profound applications for the church as a whole and for individual congregations. They are meant to 'showcase' God's glory. All of his attributes are meant to come to expression in our life together. We are his children, and should depict the family likeness; we are his temple and the architecture of our life together should be shaped by the One who indwells us.

Clearly Paul does not mean that the church shares in what are sometimes referred to as the 'incommunicable' divine attributes (omniscience, omnipresence, and similar infinite characteristics) – as though we were to be deified. Nevertheless he is praying that it will be evident in our fellowship that there is no other possible explanation for what we are than what God is. In a sense this is the burden of our Lord's great prayer for the church: our fellowship (being 'one' in the Spirit) is the fruit and reflection of the inner fellowship of God the Father, the Son and the Spirit (*John.* 17:20–23, notice the connection Jesus makes with God's glory!).

GOD'S GLORY IN CHRIST

It may seem to go without saying that God's glory will be expressed *in Christ*, the Messiah. But here Paul calls him *Christ Jesus* and thus emphasizes the deep reality of his humanity.

At the Transfiguration of our Lord, the glory of God was displayed in his humanity (*Luke.* 9:28ff.). John, who was with him, wrote that 'we have seen his glory' (*John.* 1:14). But beyond the glimpse of his glory at the Transfiguration lay the event to which it pointed – the glorification of Jesus through his death, resurrection, ascension, heavenly session, and return in majesty. In the transformed humanity of the second man and last Adam, glory took human form. His body 'sown in dishonour' was 'raised in glory' (*1 Cor.* 15:43). Now he is exalted in eternal glory.

GOD'S GLORY WITHOUT END

Thus the display of glory for which Paul longs is not merely an occasional glimpse. It will last throughout all history, for the gates of Hades will never prevail against the church that Christ is building. Then it will continue for ever – when all that belongs to Christ and has been redeemed by him will be transformed to give glorious expression to all the perfections of God the Trinity.

Amen is the word of positive response, confirmation, and affirmation used in the Old Testament. Its Hebrew root means to be faithful, reliable, true. To say *amen* means to say 'yes' to God's promises, or warnings, or praises. Jesus himself is the true Amen (*Rev.* 3:14). He alone has perfectly responded to everything God has said. In fact he has done this on our behalf. In his life of obedience he has said 'Yes' to God's law in our place – where we have said 'No'.

In his death on the cross Christ said 'Yes' to God's judgment, taking our place and being 'made sin' for us (*2 Cor.* 5:21), saying 'Yes' to receiving the judgment of God's curse so that we might not have to bear it. Indeed, says Paul, all of the promises of God are 'Yes' and 'Amen' in Christ (*2 Cor.* 1:20).

Let our own response be: Amen, and amen.

21

The One and the Many

I therefore, a prisoner for the Lord, urge you to walk in a manner worthy of the calling to which you have been called, [2]with all humility and gentleness, with patience, bearing with one another in love, [3]eager to maintain the unity of the Spirit in the bond of peace. [4]There is one body and one Spirit – just as you were called to the one hope that belongs to your call – [5]one Lord, one faith, one baptism, [6]one God and Father of all, who is over all and through all and in all. (Eph. 4:1–6)

We have come now to the hinge point of Paul's teaching. Now everything begins to change. We have read fifty-six verses of Ephesians and encountered only one command. Now exhortations flow like a swift river through 4:1–6:23. This may explain why Paul pauses, and then steps back like a long-jump athlete, as he takes his approach run to what he has to say in the following three chapters. He momentarily returns to the words with which chapter three had opened.

Paul is *a prisoner*. He is suffering for the gospel and for his fellow Christians (3:13). That is motive enough for them to pay close attention to what he says. But there is more – for Paul has received divine revelation, and has been called to communicate it to others.

While elsewhere he appeals to his apostolic office (1:1; 2:20; 3:5), here Paul is appealing to the depth of his commitment to, and the reality of his care for, the church of Jesus Christ. There is surely good reason to pay close attention to what he says. He sums it up in one exhortation, which takes him the next three chapters to work out in detail: *walk in a manner worthy of the calling with which you have been called* (4:1).

WORTHY OF THE GOSPEL?

In speaking of a lifestyle that is *worthy* of the gospel, Paul is not suggesting that we merit the grace of God. The reverse is the truth – it is God's grace that produces the new lifestyle. In this context *worthy* means 'fitting' or 'appropriate'. In Christ we are called to a lifestyle that reflects our new family name – we are 'Christ's-ones'. Our lives are to give practical expression and visible illustration to the power and reality of God's grace in us.

A central element in such a lifestyle is the harmony of our relationships with one another in the church. Ephesians 4:4–6 uses the word *one* more frequently than any other passage in the Bible – seven times in three verses. This echoes what was said in chapter two about the effect of Christ's work: he has brought together those who were previously alienated not only from God but from one another (2:12–22). Now our reconciliation to God will come to expression in the quality of our reconciliation with one another. We are to live as one because in Christ we are one!

Paul answers two basic questions in this context. (i) What does this look like in practice, and (ii) What motivation does the gospel give us to pursue it?

The motivation to a new quality of fellowship is the unity we already have in Christ (verses 3–4); practising it always requires the exercise of *love* and *humility* (verse 2).

THE PRACTICE: HUMILITY

The quality of our fellowship together as Christians depends on the exercise of *humility* and *gentleness*, *patience* and forbearance. This is a recurring theme in Paul (e.g. *Rom.* 12:3ff.; *1 Cor.* 12:14ff.; *Phil.* 2:1ff.).

Humility is not a false demeaning of ourselves. The root meaning of the Greek word is 'lowly-mindedness'. This is not a 'low self-image'. Rather it is the recognition that everything we have and are, everything we accomplish is because of the grace of Jesus Christ to us. Every gift we possess was given, not to inflate our self-importance and bolster our ego, but to enable us to minister to others as Christ has ministered to us – as a loving servant: 'what we proclaim is not ourselves, but Jesus Christ as Lord, with ourselves as your servants [bondservants] for Jesus' sake' (*2 Cor.* 4:5).

We have nothing except what we have received (*1 Cor.* 4:7). Understand this and no matter how great our gifts are, or how highly esteemed 'our ministry' is, our heads will not be inflated, nor will we count ourselves as more important than others. Indeed, the reverse will be true: for we will see that *we have received gifts* to help us to engage in humble service to others. In addition, we will recognize our need to receive the gifts Christ has given to others to enable them to serve and minister to us. This is the secret of mutual affection and esteem in the body of Christ. Furthermore, where humility reigns, tenderness and gentleness – the gentleness of our humble Saviour (*2 Cor.* 10:1) – will also be present.

Humility and unity thus go hand in glove in a fellowship that belongs to Christ. Indeed, humility turns out to be an essential ingredient in a church that is evangelistic in its existence and communal lifestyle. This was the burden of our Lord's prayer on the eve of his death:

> 'that they may all be one, just as you, Father, are in me, and I in you, that they also may be in us, so that the world may believe that you have sent me. The glory that you have given me I have given to them, that they may be one even as we are one, I in them and you in me, that they may become perfectly one, so that the world may know that you sent me and loved them even as you loved me' (*John.* 17:21–23).

PATIENCE

The *worthy* life is also characterized by *patience* and forbearance. The New Testament contains several different words that can be translated 'patience'. Paul's term here has the root meaning of being 'long-souled'. Patience means being able to take a long-term view, especially when things go wrong. Here it is appropriately coupled with *bearing with one another in love*. Christian patience involves being able to take a long-term view of a fellow Christian as a 'work in process', remembering that our Lord has been and is so patient with us. How easily we lose sight of that and treat fellow believers as though Christ had never needed to be patient with us!

UNITY

Grasp these elements in God's grace to us and we will be *eager to maintain the unity of the Spirit in the bond of peace* (verse 3). Paul loved Christians who were *eager*, enthusiastic and energetic about church fellowship. It is a priceless possession given to us in Christ. Just as we would guard a precious but fragile heirloom lest it come to any harm, so we protect Christian fellowship – the heirloom of Christ to his family – from sinister influences that might cause it damage or destroy it.

Paul helps us develop a sense of the importance of this unity by outlining its foundations, which are massive in character: *There is one body and one Spirit . . . one hope . . . one Lord, one faith, one baptism, one God and Father of all, who is over all and through all and in all* (4:4–6). Here is a unity built on a seven-fold foundation. (Is it simply a coincidence that seven is the number of perfection in the Bible?)

Christ has only *one body*. By definition its members are members of one another. He has only *one Spirit* who indwells each and every Christian believer. Think of it! At the deepest level I have in common with each of my fellow Christians this reality: the same Spirit makes our lives home for the Father and the Son (cf. *John.* 14:23). We have one and the same Master, we share the same saving trust in him, and have all received the same sign (*one baptism*). Each of us confesses the *one God*: all believers have the same *Father* – the One who rules over all things, works *through all* for our good. Our *hope* is *one*, our *faith* is *one* and our *Lord* is *one*

Could there possibly be more basic, closer, all-embracing or important unity than that?

22

Each One Has One

But grace was given to each one of us according to the measure of Christ's gift. [8]*Therefore it says, 'When he ascended on high he led a host of captives, and he gave gifts to men.'* [9]*(In saying, 'He ascended', what does it mean but that he had also descended into the lower parts of the earth?* [10]*He who descended is the one who also ascended far above all the heavens, that he might fill all things.)* [11]*And he gave the apostles, the prophets, the evangelists, the pastors and teachers,* [12]*to equip the saints for the work of ministry, for building up the body of Christ.* (Eph. 4:7–12)

Paul has been describing the foundation of church unity and explaining the chief reasons for maintaining it. It is not an optional extra, but part and parcel of our calling. We do not create it – it is the work of the Father, the Son, and the Holy Spirit. But since it is a unity we experience we must seek to sustain it – not by self-promotion but by self-denial (cf. *Phil.* 2:1–16).

There is another aspect to this unity. It does not lack variety. Rather it is the unity within a rich diversity of believers whose gifts and graces complement each other. We share in one body, says Paul – but *each one of us* functions in a different way. We trust the same Christ, we are indwelt by one and the same Spirit, we *each* have one and the same heavenly Father – yet each one of us receives *grace* – which in this context suggests a special grace-gift – from Christ, so that we can serve him and one another in a variety of different ways.

Peter expresses the same point more fully: 'As each has received a gift, use it to serve one another, as good stewards of God's varied grace [literally, multicoloured, the same adjective Paul uses in 3:10, translated 'manifold']: whoever speaks, as one who speaks oracles of God; whoever serves, as one who serves by the strength that God supplies – in order that in everything God may be glorified through Jesus Christ' (*1 Pet.* 4:10–11).

THE TRIUMPH CELEBRATION

Paul pictures this through the lenses of Psalm 68:18, which describes the Lord as a triumphant warrior.

In the ancient world a conquering general might be given a 'triumph' in honour of his victories. He would ride through the capital city of his country in a stage-managed procession – often followed by vast numbers of prisoners-of-war, with chariots and horses carrying the booty of his victory. There he would be welcomed with public acclaim and lavish displays of gratitude. These were magnificent occasions. Indeed, sometimes a slave would be positioned discreetly in the chariot of the general to say repeatedly to him '*homo es*' – remember you are only a man – lest his head be turned by the god-like worship he was receiving! Following the triumphal procession celebratory gifts – the spoils from his victories – would be distributed.

Psalm 68 describes God in such terms. He is the Mighty Warrior who has conquered all his enemies. Returning in triumph he leads his captives behind him. The victory of his death and resurrection has brought him much booty – all that he has received in conquest is set on display.

Paul saw the fulfilment of the Psalm in the ascension and exaltation of Jesus (following his victory over his enemies in his death and resurrection).

There is, however, an interesting difference between the wording of the Hebrew Psalm and Paul's citation of it: God's 'receiving gifts among men' (*Psa.* 68:18) has here become Christ *gave gifts to men* (4:8).

Other passages in Scripture help us to follow Paul's thinking here.

- On the cross Christ 'disarmed the rulers and authorities'. In his triumphal procession he 'put them to open shame, by triumphing over them . . . ' (*Col.* 2:15).

- Christ thus fulfilled the conditions of his Father's promise to give him the nations for his inheritance so that he might establish his kingdom (cf. *Psa*. 2:8).
- Once ascended, Jesus asked for the promised gift – the Holy Spirit with his gifts (*Acts* 2:33; cf. *John*. 14:16).
- Paul here describes the results: gifts are given through the Spirit to the church.

Pentecost, then, was the Triumph Day of Christ. His victory was publicly celebrated by an outpouring of gifts on the citizens in his kingdom and the soldiers in his army. He has conquered and now reigns – and one of the signs of his victory is the widespread distribution of the gifts of his grace.

DESCENT AND ASCENT

Paul notes in passing that the ascension of Christ implies an earlier descent *into the lower parts of the earth* (verse 9). This has sometimes been understood to refer to Christ's activity in between his death and resurrection. But the words most naturally suggest that his state of exaltation was preceded by a state of humiliation. First he humbled himself to become a man, a servant, and then a sin-bearer. Now he is exalted to be Lord of all things (see 1:22).

The gifts given by Christ create diversity-in-unity in the life of the church. Here Paul's focus is on 'word gifts', ministries which involve teaching and preaching the Word of God: *apostles, prophets, evangelists, pastors and teachers.*

What were these ministries and how did Paul understand their role?

APOSTLES

The word *apostle* (Greek: *apostolos*) means 'someone who has been sent'. The New Testament uses it in several different senses.

(i) *Jesus the apostle of the Father.* Frequently in John's Gospel our Lord describes the Father as the One who sent him, and himself as the One sent by the Father (*John*. 3:17, 34; 5:36, 38; 6:29, 57; 7:29; 8:42; 10:36; 11:42; 17:3, 8, 18, 21, 23, 25; 20:21). The author of Hebrews explicitly describes our Lord as 'The apostle . . . of our confession' (*Heb.* 3:1). Jesus is sent by the Father with the authority of the Father to teach the doctrine and words of the Father.

(ii) *'The Twelve' – the apostles* called by Jesus (*Luke.* 6:13) were trained by him, equipped to serve him, and sent into the world by him (*Matt.* 28:18–20). When one, Judas Iscariot, proved to be a 'devil' (*John.* 6:70) and committed suicide, the others agreed that he must be replaced (*Acts* 1:15–26). They clearly regarded the number twelve as symbolically important (an indication that Jesus was calling together the true Israel of the last days). 'The Twelve' were called by Christ and served with his authority: their word was Christ's Word to people. This explains why their letters were regarded as carrying divine authority.

The apostle Paul was added to this group (as 'one untimely born' as he puts it, *1 Cor.* 15:8). When his apostleship was attacked as inauthentic he defended it vigorously, arguing that all the necessary prerequisites for apostolic ministry were present in his life. He had seen the Lord and had been commissioned personally by him; the signs of an apostle were evident in his ministry; he had been received into the fellowship of the other members of the apostolic band (*1 Cor.* 9:1–3; 15:6, 9–10).

It is possible that in the early church some others were regarded as belonging to this group since the number twelve had symbolic rather than literal significance (with the addition of Paul, at one time there were probably at least thirteen).

Acts 14:14 refers to '*the apostles* Barnabas and Paul', while Galatians 1:19 seems to indicate that the Lord's brother James was regarded as an apostle: 'But I saw none of the other apostles except James the Lord's brother.' Paul says the risen Christ appeared to James (*1 Cor.* 15:7), thus qualifying him as an eye witness of the resurrection. In both cases the text is open to an alternative interpretation. But however many apostles there were in this sense they belonged to the foundation stage of the new community.

(iii) *Apostles of the churches.* Churches also commissioned individuals for specific tasks, which they were to accomplish in the name of the church. When Luke speaks of 'the apostles Barnabas and Paul' (*Acts* 14:14) he may be thinking of both of them as apostles of the Antioch church (although, of course, Paul also served as an apostle to the whole church). It is possibly in this sense that Andronicus and Junia(s) are described in Romans 16:7 as being 'well known to the apostles' (ESV), or 'outstanding among the apostles' (NIV). In the former case no reference to apostleship of any kind is in view. But if the latter translation is accurate these two kinsfolk of Paul had given exceptional service as apostles, or (as we might say today) as missionaries of the church.

The apostles mentioned in the well-ordered list here are apostles in sense (ii). They were given responsibility for the whole church (*Matt.* 28:18–20). Their central task was to provide authentic and authoritative witness to Christ. That witness was in turn authenticated, as Jesus' apostleship and revelation had been, by the 'signs of an apostle' (*2 Cor.* 12:12; cf. *Acts* 2:22).

PROPHETS

The position in which *prophets* appear here suggests that Paul is thinking of the special ministry that stood alongside and complemented that of apostles – to reveal God's Word, will, and purposes. We have already seen that their ministry belonged to the work of foundation building around the chief stone Jesus Christ.

Whenever God has 'expanded' the revelation by which he instructs and guides his people, he has raised up prophets. They served as the divine mouth. So in the early church, as the canon of Scripture was being expanded and eventually being completed, God gave special gifts to guide his people. Like the ministry of the apostle, this prophetic ministry was a once-for-all gift.

While this is true, we also need to recognize that in Scripture an element of all prophetic ministry was Spirit-given illumination, enabling the prophet to understand the Scriptures that had already been written, and to apply them to his own day. That element of prophetic ministry – what we might call ongoing illumination with application to individuals and the church – remains in all ministry of God's Word through which Christ speaks himself.

EVANGELISTS

It is difficult to be dogmatic about the identity and ministry of *evangelists*. But the New Testament evidence suggests that these men were not evangelists in the sense we use the term today – people with special 'evangelistic' gifts.

Only Philip is explicitly described in the New Testament as an evangelist (*Acts* 21:8). Paul urged Timothy, however, to 'do the work of an evangelist' (*2 Tim*. 4:5). What did they have in common? Both men were called in the first instance to work closely with the apostles in their ministry, and seem to have served specifically as apostolic lieutenants. Perhaps this is how we should think of the seven men who were appointed to serve on behalf of the apostles in the church at Jerusalem (*Acts* 6:1ff.). The only two of whom we hear further were engaged in apostle-like preaching ministries. They were initially set apart as apostolic lieutenants with sub-apostolic responsibilities.

If this is the case, then an evangelist had a wide-ranging commission to serve alongside or instead of an apostle. That is why they are mentioned together here.

These callings belong to the inaugural life of the New Testament church. Apostles and prophets had a foundational office (*Eph*. 2:20; 3:5); evangelists were their deputies. In the very nature of the case we do not expect these ministries to reappear in the church today.

PASTORS AND TEACHERS

Pastors and teachers were, however, clearly intended to be ongoing ministries in the church (cf. 2 *Tim*. 2:2). Here the two nouns are linked together with a single definite article ('the pastors and teachers'). This may indicate a single ministry with dual-functions. Or perhaps it suggests that pastors belonged to a larger group who were teachers without serving as pastors – all pastors teach, but not all teachers are necessarily pastors.

Here again, it is difficult to be dogmatic, and probably wise not to attempt to be – even although the interpretation of these words impinges on the practical life of our churches. What is certain, however, is that by *pastors* Paul is referring to 'elders' or 'bishops' in the church. Elsewhere he hints that while all elders are to pastor the flock, and must therefore be able to teach, some are particularly called to and gifted in the work of teaching (*1 Tim.* 5:17).

These callings focus on the ministry of God's Word. Apostles and prophets gave the Word of God in the first instance, and proclaimed it. Evangelists served with them and were to preach it. Pastors were settled in congregations and were to use it to feed the people of God. All of these ministries have a single purpose: *to equip the saints for the work of ministry, for building up the body of Christ* . . . (4:12).

As we have seen before, gifts – including these gifts – are not given to build up the self-esteem of the recipient, but the strength of the fellowship. How this happens will be the theme of what follows.

23

The Goal of Ministry

And he gave the apostles, the prophets, the evangelists, the pastors and teachers, [12]to equip the saints for the work of ministry, for building up the body of Christ, [13]until we all attain to the unity of the faith and of the knowledge of the Son of God, to mature manhood, to the measure of the stature of the fullness of Christ, [14]so that we may no longer be children, tossed to and fro by the waves and carried about by every wind of doctrine, by human cunning, by craftiness in deceitful schemes. [15]Rather, speaking the truth in love, we are to grow up in every way into him who is the head, into Christ, [16]from whom the whole body, joined and held together by every joint with which it is equipped, when each part is working properly, makes the body grow so that it builds itself up in love. (Eph. 4:11–16)

The ministry of God's Word is a gift to the church from her ascended Lord. When that Word is preached faithfully the voice of Christ is heard through the ministry of the Spirit.

The New Testament writers' view of the Old Testament was that in it God the Father 'addresses' us (present tense) 'as sons' (*Heb.* 12:5). So now, in the ministry of the Word of God Christ himself comes 'to preach peace' (*Eph.* 2:17; compare footnote 3 to the text of *Rom.* 10:14).

What fruit does this produce? How does the ascended Christ use his Word to rule over, direct, and guide the church?

There is considerable debate about exactly how Paul's words here are to be understood. Are these word-ministries given with different purposes in view, or only one?

1. In order
(i) to equip the saints
(ii) that the work of the ministry may be done
(iii) to build up the body of Christ.

or

2. In order
(i) to equip the saints for the work of ministry
(ii) to build up the body of Christ

or

3. *In order*
to equip the saints for the work of ministry so that the body of Christ may be built up.

It is difficult to decide. In practical terms the effect should be the same. Even if Paul is speaking exclusively about the work of these ministries they do equip the saints in general for their service and this leads to the strengthening of the church.

EQUIPPING THE SAINTS

The verb *to equip* was used in the medical world of restoring broken limbs. In the New Testament it is used in Matthew 4:21 to describe the fishermen-disciples getting their nets ready – cleaned and repaired – with a view to the next night's fishing.

Similarly these varied ministries of God's Word restore lives to spiritual health and strength and prepare them for future service. Thus the fellowship where the Word of God is expounded and applied in the power of the Spirit becomes a hospital for the sick and a gymnasium to build up spiritual strength and stamina. Here the ministry of the Word of God does its own healing, cleansing, transforming work on our sinful and broken lives. The result is that through its exposition the preached and received word strengthens the fellowship of believers and builds it up in unity, knowledge of Christ, spiritual height, and balanced growth until it comes to spiritual maturity.

This is the biblical understanding of the preaching of the Word of God. Its goal is not merely educational but transformational; it informs the mind in order to touch the conscience, mould the will, cleanse the affections and sanctify the whole life. The Word is thus allowed to do its own sanctifying work, as our Lord himself prayed: 'Sanctify them in the truth; your word is truth' (*John.* 17:17). This requires intensive treatment.

PAUL THE WORKING MODEL

Many of the Ephesians would have cherished a clear memory of what this kind of ministry was like. Paul had been their apostle, pastor and teacher for more than two years. When opposition to his teaching arose in the synagogue, he rented the lecture hall of Tyrannus (no prizes for guessing what nickname his students gave him if he were the teacher himself!). There Paul taught daily (*Acts* 19:9).

One family of New Testament manuscripts states that Paul did this 'from the fifth hour to the tenth' (see *Acts* 19:9, footnote 3) i.e. from 11 a.m. to 4 p.m. (the exact time would vary from summer to winter with daylight hours). While this may be a later explanatory note inserted by a scribe, it is probably an accurate reflection of what Paul did. For these were the hours when little work was done; it was 'siesta' time. So for two years (*Acts* 19:10) Paul was teaching and discussing the Scriptures and the gospel for up to five hours a day! And this for 'ordinary' Christians! No wonder 'the word of the Lord continued to increase and prevail mightily' (*Acts* 19:20).

To some (many?) Christians today this may seem excessive. But the effect of it was remarkable: 'all the residents of Asia heard the word of the Lord' (*Acts* 19:10). Clearly God's Word so transformed this group of believers that they powerfully impacted their society for Christ.

It should not surprise us that whenever there has been a spiritual quickening in the church Christians have looked for an intense diet of the ministry of the Word. Thus, in Reformation Geneva, for example, it would have been possible to hear John Calvin preach on average five, six or even seven times during the week. Were our churches to attempt to employ this simple pattern in ways that were appropriately adapted to the circumstances of modern life it might not be long before the world similarly began to take notice. Why do we seek other models? Is it because we are so malnourished that we lack the appetite and the stamina?

THE WORD AT WORK

The phrases that follow describe the fruit of such ministry.

(i) It encourages our unity (*until we all attain to the unity of the faith*). If as God's people we were together exposed to the same sanctifying truth on a regular and intensive basis, our minds and our thinking, our wills and desires, would be recalibrated to the mind and will of God.

(ii) It increases our knowledge of Christ (*the knowledge of the Son of God*). It is through his Word, opened to us in the power of the Spirit, that we get to know, understand, and love our Lord Jesus Christ. Such personal knowledge is not merely book-knowledge. Yet we have no access to knowing him apart from the revelation given to us in Scripture of who he is and what he has done.

We do not each follow a Christ forged in our own imaginations (that would be idolatry not Christianity). This is why we all need far more exposure than most of us receive to God's Word rightly interpreted and applied in the power of the Spirit.

With hours of that exposure each week (plus additional instruction at times in their own homes – see *Acts* 20:20!), the Ephesians must have well understood what Paul meant.

(iii) It leads to spiritual maturity *(to mature manhood, to the measure of the stature of the fullness of Christ*). Maturity means becoming more like Christ, becoming full of Christ; it comes from letting the Word of Christ dwell in us richly (*Col.* 3:16).

STABILITY AND INTEGRITY

Paul goes on to spell out the practical implications of this maturity.

We grow in stability (verse 14). The ministry of the Word enables us to mature so that we are *no longer . . . children*. Children grow in stages. As infants they are unsteady on their feet and easily knocked over; they are readily distracted; they lack the necessary experience to distinguish the insignificant from the really valuable; they are easily taken in by the superficial; they find it difficult to see things in the long term.

The same is true spiritually. Immature believers are today exposed to 'the latest thing', the most recent 'wind of doctrine' that blows through the evangelical church. The marketing of literature, television preachers, seminars, videos, DVDs and the like almost necessitates novelty. The pride of the human heart does not like to be thought old-fashioned. A new wind blows through each year, a hurricane every few years. Many are swept off their feet by teaching that may begin with an open but misinterpreted Bible and ends with a deceived mind.

But the prolonged, intensive, faithful exposition of God's Word delivers us from immaturity. Indeed, as the psalmist notes, knowing Scripture can give us more understanding than our teachers and make us wiser than our enemies (*Psa.* 119:98–99). Study and meditation, application and obedience develop in us the ability to see clearly, to distinguish between what is true and false, and also between what is good and what is really best. We are then not deceived by false teaching. The truth of the gospel makes our spiritual antennae sensitive. The Word seeps into our instincts so that we sense the superficial and detect teaching that is sinister or dangerous (*human cunning . . . craftiness . . . deceitful schemes*, verse 14). Far from being immature, spiritual teenagers as it were, driven by our emotions, attracted by spiritual 'spin', shaped by the passing trends of peer pressure, we live by the Word of God and grow strong.

We develop integrity (verse 15). *Speaking the truth in love* (literally: 'truthing in love') becomes instinctive to us. While falsehood was a characteristic of the old life (4:25), truth, integrity, and reality are the marks of disciples of Christ the Truth (*John.* 14:6). Pretence and hypocrisy have no place in the new community of grace. Moreover, *truth* is always set in the context of *love* because it is never only a matter of speech and words, but of spirit and motive. Truth and love together express the balance of the mature Christian and lead to growth in a church fellowship.

We progress in unity (verse 16). Christians who are already united to Christ and therefore to one another grow nearer to and more and more like Christ and correspondingly nearer to one another in his body the church. Paul describes this with vivid imagery. Like a human body, the church is held together with *joints.* Only when every part is *working properly* does healthy growth take place. But where there is a wise and nourishing ministry of the Word it will happen. And it will do so almost like a youngster growing to maturity in his or her own body – which seems to 'grow itself': *the body builds itself up in love.*

Often our churches do not seem to be growing. Stunted fellowship is almost always caused by a lack of either truth or love – sadly sometimes by both. Where the central ministries of the Word are lacking, the knowledge of the *truth* will be diminished and the ability to develop maturity impoverished. Where there is not thoroughgoing submission to the Word *love* will be lacking and any growth will be misshapen and unlike Christ.

But where, under the ministry of the Word, truth and love go hand in hand, growth is assured and grace prevails.

24

New Life for Old

Now this I say and testify in the Lord, that you must no longer walk as the Gentiles do, in the futility of their minds. [18]They are darkened in their understanding, alienated from the life of God because of the ignorance that is in them, due to their hardness of heart. [19]They have become callous and have given themselves up to sensuality, greedy to practice every kind of impurity. [20]But that is not the way you learned Christ! – [21]assuming that you have heard about him and were taught in him, as the truth is in Jesus, [22]to put off your old self, which belongs to your former manner of life and is corrupt through deceitful desires, [23]and to be renewed in the spirit of your minds, [24]and to put on the new self, created after the likeness of God in true righteousness and holiness. (Eph. 4:17–24)

God made man as his image and called him to exercise royal dominion over the whole creation to manifest God's glory in it. But man fell and with him the whole creation was subjected to futility (*Rom.* 8:20). Instead of reaching their intended destination, man and creation fell short of the glory for which they had been created (*Rom.* 3:23). Consequently 'the whole creation has been groaning . . . until now' (*Rom.* 8:22).

But even as Paul was composing his letter to the Ephesians a new *now* had already dawned – the 'now' of the resurrection of Christ and the gift of the Spirit; the 'now' of 'the last days', the inauguration of the new creation. God had now put into effect his largely hidden plan (cf. 1:9) to bring everything together under the dominion of the Last Adam (cf. *Gen.* 1:26–28). At the end, Christ the Second Man and Last Adam will complete that task and do what the First Man

Adam failed to do, namely to lead the cosmos in tribute to God the Creator (cf. *1 Cor.* 15:20–28).

We have repeatedly seen that to this grand design there were three obstacles, which God has now overthrown in Christ: the powers of darkness, the spiritual death of individuals, and the alienation of humanity. While not yet finalized, God has already begun to express this triumph in the life of the church. It is the sphere in which the multi-dimensional wisdom of God has been put on display (3:10). Indeed it is in the church that God's character is intended to be most clearly seen. It is in the church that the world is to see the glory of Christ and come to believe in him (*John.* 17:17–23). This is why the church's unity and growth to stability – through the ministry of the Word (4:1–16) – are so important.

Now Paul turns to the practical outworking of this and indicates in some detail how profoundly the gospel transforms the life of the community of grace and its members. Whereas in the earlier sections almost everything he had said was in the indicative mood, now we find that imperative follows imperative in quick succession. Having sunk deep foundations into God's grace ('we are his workmanship') he now unfolds what it means for us to be 'created in Christ Jesus for good works' (2:10).

Paul's imperatives come so thick and fast that we might make the mistake of thinking they came to mind in random fashion. The reverse is the truth. They have a unifying motif and a simple form.

The *motif* is that of walking (4:17; 5:2; 5:8; 5:15) which is a biblical metaphor for lifestyle ('walking' in God's ways; cf. *Gen.* 5:22; 6:9; 17:1; *Deut* 8:6; *Psa.* 1:1). In fact this whole section is rooted in the overarching exhortation to Christians to walk in a way that befits their calling (4:1).

The basic *form* of teaching in this whole section is a simple one:

- We are no longer to live as we once did as the 'old man'

because

- We no longer are the 'old man' we once were,

but

- We are to become in practical expression the 'new man' we now are in Christ.

Thus the rest of Ephesians 4 can be summarized as follows:

1. 4:17–19: What we once were
2. 4:20–24: What we now are
3. 4:25–32: What we are to become

THE PAST – WHAT WE ONCE WERE

We *must no longer walk as the Gentiles do* (verse 17). Paul's language expresses his sense of authority as an apostle. He speaks emphatically: *I say and testify in the Lord.* Paul wishes to emphasise what follows. His words constitute the solemn and binding testimony of an apostle speaking as the representative of Christ the Lord, and with his full authority.

Paul does not spare us in his acute analysis of our sinful condition. Notice the flow of his logic:

Hardness of heart leads to
Ignorance which involves being
Alienated from the life of God which leads to our being
Darkened in our understanding with the result that we become
Callous and
Given up to sensuality and thus
Greedy to practise every kind of impurity (verses 18–19)

In three verses Paul summarises the teaching he gives at greater length in Romans 1:18–32. It is sobering conscience-probing analysis. It describes the true nature of the world apart from Christ. It is a catalogue of what we all are by nature. He puts a spiritual stethoscope to our hearts to let us hear that its beat is out of control.

Apart from Christ's work the cosmos was destined to futility (*Rom.* 8:20). Apart from God's special revelation the human race (= Gentiles, those who have never had the special revelation of grace) was condemned to futility. Its every effort to solve the jigsaw puzzle of existence was doomed to frustration. Satisfaction and fulfilment sought in the creation rather than in the Creator, worshipping it rather than him, became the high road to eternal disappointment.

While unbelievers may affirm that their rejection of the Christian faith is fundamentally a matter of intellectual integrity, Paul stresses that the rebellious disposition of the heart drives and directs the understanding. Thus the Scriptures tell us something about the unbeliever which he or she tends to deny, suppress and repress – namely that their rejection of God runs contrary to what they know 'deep down' to be true (cf. *Rom.* 1:18–23). Since this was once true of us we need to be reminded to be patient in our witness and to pray for the illuminating and regenerating work of the Spirit as we bear witness to Christ.

THE PRESENT – WHO WE NOW ARE

This ungodly pattern was not *the way you learned Christ* says Paul (4:20). His language is, to say the least, unusual. How do we *learn* a person? We learn subjects and facts, but we 'learn about' people. Is this simply a different way of saying 'learn from or about' Christ?

Perhaps. But becoming a Christian involves more than learning *about* Christ. It is *learning Christ* in the sense that we come to know him. In learning about him, we come to trust and love him. To live *as the Gentiles do* would be to have learned nothing! It would be to repudiate Christ!

Paul assumes better of the Ephesian Christians (verse 21). This is not how they were taught! That is not the life that is 'worthy of the calling' with which they were called into union with Christ!

What, then, were they taught *as the truth is in Jesus* (verse 21)? In what practical ways had they *learned Christ*? Notice first the structure and logic of what Paul says:

You were taught:

- *to put off your old self which belongs to your former manner of life and is corrupt through deceitful desires* (literally 'to put off you, according to the former conduct, the old man, the one being corrupted according to the lusts of deceit')

and

- *to be renewed in the spirit of your minds*

and

- *to put on the new self, created after the likeness of God.*

This is a key statement and it takes us to the heart of how Paul understands what it means to be a Christian.

The Ephesians were taught *to put off, to be renewed,* and *to put on*. What do these things mean. When and how did or do they happen?

WHAT HAPPENED TO ME?

According to Paul when we come to faith we believe 'into' Christ and are united to him by the Spirit. We are now 'in Christ' (his favourite way of describing the Christian believer). This determines everything about our lives. But what does it mean?

By nature we are members of the family of which Adam was the original father. Paul also thinks of him as our representative Head. By nature we are 'in Adam' – we fell in him and experience the consequences of this in our lifestyle and destiny (*Rom.* 5:12–21; *1 Cor.* 15:22).

When we trust in Christ the ties that bind us to Adam are broken and we are 'adopted' into a new family and culture. We now belong to Christ, the new Adam and representative Head of God's people. Because we are 'in Christ' everything he did for us becomes ours.

If this is now the fundamental truth about our identity, we need to learn to live in the light of it. That is what it means to *learn Christ* and to be *taught in him* the *truth that is in Jesus* (4:21). It means to understand what has happened to us when we became Christians and what implications arise for our lives. It means being *renewed in the spirit of your minds* (verse 23) – so that we think about ourselves in a completely new and different way:

(i) The *old self* has been put away (verse 22). Paul speaks literally about 'the old *man* or *person*'. As in Romans 5:12–6:14 (cf. 6:6 especially) the 'old man' does not merely denote my earlier life but that earlier life seen as constituted in Adam, under the powers of the old world. The influences of my past life linger on and need to be resisted; but I am no longer 'in Adam'. I am no longer a prisoner of the old order.

(ii) The *new self* (literally, 'the new *man* or *person*') has been put on. This means more than that my life has changed and become new.

Earlier (2:15) Paul had spoken about the way in which in Christ 'one new man' has been created. 'New' thus means 'belonging to the new age inaugurated by the resurrection of Christ'.

Christ himself became 'the first new man', 'the man of the new age', in his resurrection. When we trusted in Christ, our ties to the old Adam were broken and we *put off* the old man. In being united to the new Adam, by faith and in the power of the Holy Spirit, we also *put on* the new man.

The concepts here are bigger than simply saying we lived an old life and we now live a new life. In our new life in Christ the destiny for which Adam was created will now come to fulfilment. We are *created* again *after the likeness of God* (cf. *Gen.* 1:26–28). His image, marred and broken by the fall, is restored. We reflect once again his character and glory – we are [re]*created . . . in true righteousness and holiness* (verse 24).

Clearly it takes a lifetime to work out into our thinking and living all the implications of this truth. But Paul has given notice that the gospel is a message of cosmic proportions. It is no small thing to become a Christian.

We do not naturally think about ourselves this way. We need to be taught it. And we need to learn it. Better, we need to *learn Christ*. That will lead us to discover how our old identity has gone; we have been given a new identity in Christ.

Our lives can never be the same again.

25

Become What You Are

Therefore, having put away falsehood, let each one of you speak the truth with his neighbour, for we are members one of another. [26]*Be angry and do not sin; do not let the sun go down on your anger,* [27]*and give no opportunity to the devil.* [28]*Let the thief no longer steal, but rather let him labour, doing honest work with his own hands, so that he may have something to share with anyone in need.* [29]*Let no corrupting talk come out of your mouths, but only such as is good for building up, as fits the occasion, that it may give grace to those who hear.* [30]*And do not grieve the Holy Spirit of God, by whom you were sealed for the day of redemption.* [31]*Let all bitterness and wrath and anger and clamour and slander be put away from you, along with all malice.* [32]*Be kind to one another, tender-hearted, forgiving one another, as God in Christ forgave you.* (Eph. 4:25–32)

To be a Christian means to be united to the risen and exalted Christ. We now share in the new creation of which he is the firstfruits. As Christians we have put off the old man and have put on the new man. We no longer live as we once did (4:17) because the person we once were – united to Adam – is no more.

The powers of a new age have been released into our lives. We are no longer living in the domain where sin reigns but in Christ where grace and righteousness reign! As part of God's new creation we now possess a new identity reflecting the righteousness and holiness of God (4:24).

Paul famously makes the same point in 2 Corinthians 5:17: 'If any one is in Christ – new creation!' It is not only that I am inwardly renewed as an individual; rather a whole new order of reality has arrived. The dawn of the new age has come over the horizon from the future. I am no longer living in death and the dominion of sin but in life and the reign of grace. The implications of this are monumental.

It is to these implications that Paul now turns. They follow the logic that always marks his teaching on growing in holiness. Our new identity has come through union with Christ in his death and resurrection. The new life, which flows from it, involves putting away or putting to death (*Col.* 3:5) everything which is unlike Christ, and putting on or developing graces, which reflect the resurrection power of the Lord. We are being gradually transformed into his likeness and image (*Col.* 3:12, cf. 3:10).

PUTTING OFF AND PUTTING ON

A lengthy series of imperatives now follows (4:25–32). They give detailed instructions, and in doing so highlight two important principles of sanctification:

(i) There is no progress in holiness unless we put away what belongs to the old lifestyle *and* put on what belongs to the new one – simultaneously. This principle grows inevitably out of our union with Christ.

To attempt to do one without the other leads only to failure. Putting away the old lifestyle is not the same as growing more like Christ. For that we must put on the lifestyle of the new age, the dispositions produced in us by the Spirit. Without that positive counterpart our sanctification will have a metallic ring and express itself in a brittle and unattractive life.

On the other hand it is fatal to think that we can grow in positive likeness to Christ without rigorously rejecting lingering sinful dispositions and habits. That would be like seeking to plant flowers in a garden infested by weeds – without either weeding or using weed killer.

(ii) The fact that Paul issues these imperatives – specific commands which tell us in very concrete ways what the will of God is – underlines for us that the New Testament does not dispense with the need for God's law. Granted the Ten Commandments come to us now through Christ who has redeemed us, not simply from the hands of Moses, they remain the law of the same God. Indeed it is the ministry of the Spirit to write God's law on our hearts rather than abolish its requirements (*Jer.* 31:33; cf. *Heb.* 8:10; 10:16).

This should not surprise us. We have already seen that the substance of the Ten Commandments was in essence the original blueprint for man's life. It reflected the way we were originally meant to function. Only later, in the context of sin on the one hand, and the progress of redemptive history on the other, did this need to be expressed in written form and shaped in a negative way (hence the repeated stress in the Decalogue on 'You shall not . . . ').

NEW LIFE PATTERNS

How, then, should we live as part of the new creation in Christ? The basic principle is that growing in grace involves both *displacement* (of sinful habits and lifestyle) and *replacement* (by Christ-like graces and habits).

Paul gives a series of exhortations and relates each of them to their foundation in God's gracious working through the gospel:

1. *Truth must replace falsehood* (verse 25). Why? Because we have been brought together into one body in Christ (2:16), and have been called to maintain the unity already ours in the union we share together in Christ. A lack of integrity in the body inevitably causes it to malfunction. Lies, pretence, hypocrisy – these are all viruses against which our fellowships need protection. They must be resisted.

2. *Anger that is righteous – must replace anger that controls us.* Anger is expressed righteously only when it does not dominate us, or become an obsession to us (verse 26). It is right to get angry about some things. But remaining angry when the sun goes down (i.e. at the end of the day) is a sign that instead of expressing right judgment, anger has mastered us.

Notice Paul's underlying concern here – believers must not allow the devil a foothold in their relationships with one another. The more we allow alienation to fester in our anger the more opportunity we give Satan to twist hearts, spread rumours, stimulate self-justification and spawn party spirit. Unlike our Lord, Satan has many things in us on which he can land and engage in his destroying work (contrast *John.* 14:30).

3. *Generosity must replace theft.* Not only is theft forbidden, but the commandment 'You shall not steal' is obeyed only when we express its (positive) opposite (verse 28).

We share the tendency of the man who asked Jesus to identify the 'neighbour' whom God's law commanded him to love (*Luke* 10:25ff.). He wanted to place limits on his responsibility. So here. We imagine that so long as we do not commit theft we have kept the law. But God is concerned about the goal of the commandment: giving generously, as those who have received generously. The law is given a deeper dimension in Christ – for he has shown us what it means to give not only generously but sacrificially.

Everything Adam and Eve had in the Garden of Eden was a gift from God, to be enjoyed and shared. But rather than receiving, sharing, and giving, they wanted more – fruit that did not belong to them.

The key here is to learn that nothing is our own; all is the Lord's. We are not owners of anything but stewards of everything.

4. *The language of blessing must replace that of cursing* (verse 29). Words can poison and thus be *corrupting*. We must abstain. For some it is not difficult to refrain from cursing. But it is a greater thing to know how to use words for encouragement, *such as is good for building up* rather than tearing down. Grace teaches us how to say the helpful thing at just the right time.

It is out of the heart that the mouth speaks (*Luke* 6:45). The new heart given to us by the Holy Spirit will come to expression on our lips. For a heart desire to serve others works hard to find the right words.

Paul adds that – unlike ancient Israel (see *Isa.* 63:10) – we must not *grieve the Spirit* (verse 30) by the words that come from our lips – words marked by criticism and expressing a complaining spirit.

This expression is one of the clearest indications in the New Testament that we are to think of the Spirit in personal terms – he is someone who can be *grieved*. Why should our sin *grieve the Spirit*? Because we have been *sealed with* him with a view to our final salvation (cf. 1:13). To live as though that were a matter of indifference to us is to wound him deeply. He has united us to Christ in whom God has 'blessed' (or 'spoken well') of us (1:3). If the Father through the Spirit has thus spoken his blessing on us in his Son, how perverse we are if we do not speak well of one another (cf. *James* 3:9–10). How grieved the Spirit must sometimes be!

So *bitterness . . . wrath . . . anger . . . clamour . . . slander* – these grieve the Spirit, and should grieve our spirits too, if we are in tune with him.

5. *Kindness must replace animosity* (verse 31). Again Paul hints that this is not something that can be fabricated, certainly not in the long term. For *being kind* comes from a tender heart. Kindness to others is rooted in our own sense of how much we have needed the kindness of God, and received it from him (2:7). We have been forgiven; we should learn to forgive.

The Lord Jesus was kind; he has been kind to me. My refusal or failure to be kind to others would be a sure sign I had never really tasted his kindness. If I had, I would want to pass it on.

The new life Paul describes here may seem at first sight disappointingly mundane and unspectacular. These verses do not describe mighty deeds wrought in great power, but humble lives transformed by the Holy Spirit.

The testimony of Augustine, one of the towering figures of church history and of all western thought, is telling in this regard. Having lived for self, dabbled in false cults, pursued the satisfaction of his desires, he was – eventually – brought to faith in Christ in the city of Milan, whose Bishop was the eloquent Ambrose. Recalling on one occasion how he had come to faith, Augustine reflects on the influence of Ambrose: 'It was not your great teaching – I scarcely expected to find that in the Christian Church in any case – *but that you were kind to me.*'

Why did this impress him? Perhaps it authenticated his preaching. Perhaps it helped Augustine to see and believe that the God and Saviour of such a man as Ambrose of Milan must himself be kind.

And if kind, then perhaps this Saviour whom Ambrose preached would be willing to accept even Augustine, pardon his sins and transform his life.

So it was. Perhaps the same thing would happen through our lives . . . if these things were true of us.

26

Walking in Love

Therefore be imitators of God, as beloved children. [2]*And walk in love, as Christ loved us and gave himself up for us, a fragrant offering and sacrifice to God.* [3]*But sexual immorality and all impurity or covetousness must not even be named among you, as is proper among saints.* [4]*Let there be no filthiness nor foolish talk nor crude joking, which are out of place, but instead let there be thanksgiving.* [5]*For you may be sure of this, that everyone who is sexually immoral or impure, or who is covetous (that is, an idolater), has no inheritance in the kingdom of Christ and God.*
[6]*Let no one deceive you with empty words, for because of these things the wrath of God comes upon the sons of disobedience.*
[7]*Therefore do not associate with them;* [8]*for at one time you were darkness, but now you are light in the Lord. Walk as children of light.* (Eph. 5:1–8)

Christians are different. They are called to 'walk in a manner worthy' of their calling (4:1). That means living differently from others (4:17ff.), because we *are* different – we have put off the old man and put on the new man (4:22, 24). More than that, an ongoing renewal is taking place in us.

Now Paul introduces a further development of this theme. In 5:1–21 he encourages his readers to *walk in love* (5:2–8), *walk as children of light* (5:8–14), and *walk . . . as wise* (5:15–21).

In fact these three elements (love, light, wisdom) are all expressive of the character of God himself and are summed up in the single idea with which the chapter begins: *Therefore be imitators of God, as beloved children.*

The fifth commandment in the Decalogue ('Honour your father and your mother', *Exod.* 20:12) implicitly taught a child the meaning of commandments six to ten. Honouring parents, modelling their lives on their love for, and obedience to, the Lord and his Word – this encapsulated for children all that was necessary for spiritual faithfulness.

Children are mimics. They learn by watching and sensing as well as by hearing specific explanations and instructions. Here Paul transposes this idea to a higher key. Since God is our heavenly Father, we are to model our life and our dispositions on him. Imitate your Father! Moreover, we not only have the perfect model to imitate; we have every incentive to do so because we are his 'beloved children'. 'In love he predestined us for adoption through Jesus Christ' (1:4–5).

So we are commanded, first of all: 'walk in love'.

COMMANDED TO LOVE!

Paul *commands* us to love! He gives us incentive, motivation, and even points us to the resources (God's love for us) on which to draw; but, nevertheless, he gives us a command – what James calls 'the royal law, 'You shall love . . . ' (*James* 2:8; cf. *John.* 15:12).

Loving others is not an optional extra in the Christian life but a requirement. It does not depend on the whims of our emotions but on understanding God's Word, on the commitment of our will and the devotion of our heart. It is deliberate obedience, not an inexplicable urge that overtakes us.

Christians are called to imitate the love of God, which has been expressed in and through Jesus (*as Christ loved us*, verse 2). Paul is even more specific: this love is to be modelled on the sacrificial love of Jesus, on his willingness to give *himself up for us, a fragrant offering and sacrifice* out of love for and obedience to the Father. Later, Paul will urge husbands to love their wives in this way (5:25). But this is the model for all love, for all believers, for all circumstances, for all time.

LOVE AT WORK

Paul's description of how love is to work in the fellowship at Ephesus is also arresting. It is the outworking of the life of the new man in

Christ: shunning the un-Christ-like while positively expressing his grace. What he has to say about loving seems to be dominated by those things that love shuns (cf. *1 Cor.* 13:4–6a). But this, as always, is set within a positive context.

Love acts in a way that is *proper among saints* (verse 3) – in a saintly way! This means, among other things, that it engages in avoidance of sin to such a degree that its language never stimulates interest in the sinful. So *sexual immorality and all impurity or covetousness must not be named . . . no filthiness nor foolish talk nor crude joking . . .* As he later indicates at length, Paul knows that the Christian life involves spiritual warfare (cf. 6:10–20), and – as in all wars – 'careless talk costs lives'.

This gives a needed spiritual health warning for Christians in the West, and increasingly in every continent. The media daily bombard our lives with words and images which express all of the things Paul mentions. We can easily be desensitized to the sinful by what has become 'normal' in our society. The danger, then, is that we begin to think of the morally abnormal as normal, and of things that tend to cause moral carelessness as matters of indifference. Christ-like love banishes the salacious. Smut should be suffocated in the holy atmosphere of our fellowship.

Paul is very specific – a characteristic of the way he always deals with the ongoing patterns of the old lifestyle. There are some things that should never be topics of conversation among believers (*not even be named*), far less given free rein.

Interestingly, just as Paul's general exhortation to imitate God (5:1) echoes the fifth commandment, these words echo commandments six to ten. He is not saying anything new. The new commandment is the old one. Yet it has become new (*1 John.* 2:8–9); it is specifically the love of Christ and the inward energy of the Spirit that constrain us to fulfil the commands (*Rom.* 8:3–4). They are thus old, yet also 'new' in Christ – new in the sense that now we have the full resources of Christ for obedience to them. New also, perhaps, in the degree to which they penetrate to the basic motives of our hearts, calling us to purity and obedience in desire as well as in deed. Paul could hardly make clearer that the new life is a pattern of existence that develops out of the new heart on which the law of God has been written (*Jer.* 31:33; *Heb.* 8:10; 10:16).

INCENTIVES TO HOLINESS

Paul now gives us a series of incentives for distancing ourselves from the old lifestyle and the conversation, interests and activities of the world.

- Such interest and talk is *out of place*. It does not 'fit' us any longer (verse 4).
- The actions to which it leads disqualify us from any *inheritance in the kingdom* of Christ. We cannot be heirs of a holy kingdom while we are living as citizens of a sinful one (verse 5).
- To engage in this lifestyle is evidence that we have been deceived – blinded to the truth of the matter, taking the bait that hides the hook that will ensnare us (verse 6).
- Such behaviour and conversation actually merits *the wrath of God*. This is the destiny of those whose lives are characterized by disobedience rather than by faith (verse 6).

What should we then do? First, a 'do not': *do not associate with them* (verse 7). Paul does not mean that we should leave the world altogether (*1 Cor.* 5:10). Rather, we should have no natural 'connection' with ungodliness – spiritually we have nothing in common with such darkness.

We once *were darkness* (verse 8) – and had everything in common with those who live in it. Now we are *light in the Lord* – and have nothing in common. Our new task is to invade the darkness with light.

The language here is arresting. We not only lived in darkness: we *were darkness*. The darkness was within, and was therefore inescapably part of our being. We lived in it; it lived in us. We could not see in or beyond the darkness until the light of the glory of God in Christ shone into our hearts (*2 Cor.* 4:4–6). We looked into darkness with spiritually darkened eyes. If the light within you is darkness how great is the darkness, said our Lord (*Matt.* 6:23). And how great the tragedy – that we thought it was light!

No wonder Paul urges those who once were darkness to avoid returning to it or engaging in conversation appropriate to it! To do so shows either that we have never been converted or that we have a very weak grasp of what conversion really involves.

Paul thus fills out his characteristic pattern for sanctification. We are no longer what we once were, therefore we do not live as we once did. 'Not this, but that' is now the rhythm of the steps of the godly man or woman.

But again Paul surprises us, for the specific antithesis he draws to unseemly conversation is unexpected: *instead let there be thanksgiving'* (verse 4).

THE THANKFUL APPROACH

Have you ever thought that *thanksgiving* might be a remedy for unsanctified conversation and thoughts of sexual sin, impurity, covetous desires and heart idolatry that lie behind it?

What is the logic here? It is spiritually insightful and very practical. When we see people and things in the light of God and his Word, and express gratitude to him for his good and gracious gifts, we cannot simultaneously illegitimately desire them. Nor can we be simultaneously thankful and self-full. Uncontrolled speech, sinful desires and actions are driven away by this grace! Ask 'How can I be thankful about this?' and you have taken the first step to a purer life.

To *walk in love* means to leave the world of darkness for the world of light. It means walking in the light. This is the theme Paul now develops.

27

Walking in the Light

For at one time you were darkness, but now you are light in the Lord. Walk as children of light [9] *(for the fruit of light is found in all that is good and right and true),* [10] *and try to discern what is pleasing to the Lord.* [11] *Take no part in the unfruitful works of darkness, but instead expose them.* [12] *For it is shameful even to speak of the things that they do in secret.* [13] *But when anything is exposed by the light, it becomes visible,* [14] *for anything that becomes visible is light. Therefore it says,*

'Awake, O sleeper, and arise from the dead,
and Christ will shine on you.' (Eph. 5:8–14)

To be *in the Lord* is to belong to a new world, to inhabit a new kingdom in which we become new men and women. In this new kingdom, new powers are at work in us – the powers of the Spirit of the crucified, risen, ascended, reigning and returning Christ. Once we were in the darkness. Worse, the darkness was in us – we *were darkness*. Now we have been drawn into the light, illuminated by Christ the Light of the world. More, we have been invaded and transformed by Christ the Light. In the Lord we *are light*!

Here again we are confronted by the Pauline pattern for Christian growth: since you are new men and women in Christ, no longer live as though you were still old. *Therefore* . . . Do not . . . but do . . . ; put off . . . but put on; say no . . . but also say yes.

The pattern appears again here. We *are light* in Christ; we must learn to *walk as children of light*. The fruit of this will be *all that is good and right and true* (verse 9).

Light produces fruit! As the light of Christ shines on our lives it transforms us. Natural growth in the botanical and horticultural realm depends on a variety of influences: soil, rain, sun. Without the combination there will be no growth. So it is for the Christian. Growth is produced by God's multi-dimensional activities – through his working in providence, for example. But always his light is needed – light that illumines our understanding; light from his Word that banishes the darkness in our thinking, willing, and feeling; light that reproduces itself in us as 'naturally' as fruit growing on a tree – fruit that is *good and right and true*.

In a sense Paul is simply summarizing what he had earlier written to the Galatians about the 'fruit of the Spirit' (*Gal.* 5:22–23). The gospel produces transformed character whose distinguishing mark is the through-and-through graciousness which comes from living in the company of the Light of the world.

As Christ illumines our lives the darkness that remains in us is exposed and banished. Yes, there will be struggle, pain, failure on the way. But Paul's point is that these qualities are not 'worked up' by us, by our strenuous efforts to be morally upright. Rather, in and through the struggle the light of grace is being reflected in our lives, from within.

DISCERNING GOD'S WILL

One of the marks of the *children of light* is that they will *try to discern what is pleasing to the Lord* (verse 10). *Discern* here translates a favourite verb in Paul's vocabulary. Its background lies in the idea of examining and verifying something. It is used of examining metals in order to detect impurities and prove genuineness. In this way it comes to mean discernment, the ability to evaluate. Despite the *ESV* translation, there is no verb *try to* but a present participle of the verb to *discern*. So Paul is saying *Walk as children of the light . . .* discerning *what is pleasing to the Lord.*

Here Paul gives us a helpful directive on the subject of guidance. How do I discover the will of God with respect to my life? The answer is: Discover what pleases him.

How do we do that? God has already shown us what pleases him – in the life and ministry and obedience of our Lord. He has told us what pleases him – in his Word, the Holy Scriptures. The life of discernment is, therefore, a Word-focussed and Word-directed life, which develops a Word-saturated mind.

On the negative side, Paul warns us against participation in the *works of darkness* (verse 11). Notice again the contrasting language he uses (as he does also in Galatians and Romans). The gospel of light produces *fruit*; its effects appear with a spiritual naturalness, not by artificial forcing or feeding. By contrast darkness produces *works* – effort, toil, a sinful striving. Sin, at the end of the day, exhausts and then kills us. It is *unfruitful* – it produces the 'body of death' (*Rom.* 7:24) and destroys the soil in which grace and lasting pleasure grows.

EXPOSING THE DARKNESS

But the Christian cannot stop there. His or her life is not merely a matter of darkness-avoidance. It includes darkness-exposure. One cannot *be* light without exposing the darkness. Christians do not, as it were, 'switch on the light' when necessary; they *are light* and are to 'let' their light shine (*Matt.* 5:16). As Christians we 'shine' because we *are* Christ's.

But what does darkness-exposure involve? Those who shine as light in the world by definition do not share in the darkness. The way they live *exposes* the darkness with its *secret and shameful* deeds (verse 12). The word combination here is striking. Paul understands that by definition unbelievers live in the darkness. They have secrets that, if brought to the light, will be seen for what they really are. When anything becomes visible, the truth about it *is exposed by the light*. Think of someone taking a garment outside the store in order to see its 'true colours' under natural rather than artificial light. In the same way, the light of the lives of saints shows up the sin around them in its true colours.

How daunting, yet also encouraging, this teaching is. It is daunting – because Paul indicates that our lives shed more light than we realize and lead to reactions and responses we might never anticipate. Sometimes these are deeply hostile, like the tantrums of a child when its naughtiness is exposed. But the apostle's teaching is also encouraging – because it is what we *are* in Christ (not only what we *do*) that shines as light in the darkness. We have no interest in talking about the shameful thoughts, desires, and deeds of sin. Those who live in the light have better things to talk about, think about, and to enjoy!

INTO THE LIGHT

Paul had seen this principle of evangelism at work in his own life. In the Acts of the Apostles his conversion is set within the context of the courageous witness of Stephen. But behind the account of Stephen's trial and death lies an almost unnoticed fact. He and Saul almost certainly belonged to the same Jewish synagogue group (*Acts* 6:9), and indeed to the same generation.

The young Saul of Tarsus – who strived so earnestly to excel others in everything he did (*Phil.* 3:4–6) – had probably witnessed the transformation of Stephen's life. He had certainly heard Stephen speak about Christ. Perhaps he found it impossible to contradict the power and reality of what he heard and saw (*Acts* 6:10). Stephen was like light: Luke comments that 'his face was like the face of an angel' (*Acts* 6:15). Saul must have felt himself exposed, even if he could not articulate exactly why. He reacted in fury, like an infant screaming because it does not get its own will and knows no other way to express itself.

So it often is. We should never forget that as we live our lives as light in the world. Quiet and consistent godliness can provoke deep anger and hostility. It is 'hard to kick against the goads' (*Acts* 26:14)!

SLEEPER AWAKE!

This little section concludes with what modern translations set as a quotation, introduced by the words *it says* (verse 14). But unlike other quotations introduced by 'it says' (e.g. 4:8; cf. *Jas.* 4:6) these words are not found in the Scriptures.

The words clearly echo Isaiah 60:1–2. Perhaps Paul means that, in terms of the coming of Christ as the fulfilment of prophecy, this is what the text *says* or what Christ *says* to us through it. Or, possibly, these words come from a hymn composed on the basis of Isaiah's words. Paul had been in the area of Ephesus for three years. He would have known the songs customarily sung by the Christian fellowships there.

In either case these words express the glorious, powerful call of Christ himself in the gospel. They are a reworking of the teaching Paul had already given in Ephesians 2:1ff. We were dead in sin; Christ called us – deaf and dead though we were – through his deafness-penetrating, death-reversing word. We heard his voice and arose to follow him. We once walked in darkness, we now enjoy the light, just as he himself said: 'I am the light of the world. Whoever follows me will not walk in darkness, but will have the light of life' (*John*. 8:12).

If you are *light in the Lord* – Shine!

28

Walking in Wisdom

> *Look carefully then how you walk, not as unwise but as wise,* [16]*making the best use of the time, because the days are evil.* [17]*Therefore do not be foolish, but understand what the will of the Lord is.* (Eph. 5:15–17)

It used to be commonplace to speak about 'the Christian walk'. It is the theme of this extensive section in Ephesians (4:1ff.). Paul uses the verb *walk* several times (4:1, 17; 5:2, 8, 15). The idea is not new to Paul, however. Jesus had already spoken of two gates, broad and narrow, from which we have to choose, opening into two paths, likewise broad and narrow, leading either to destruction or to life (*Matt.* 7:13–14). But even before our Lord, the great and decisive spiritual choices of God's covenant with his people had been regularly described as a choice between two paths and two ways of walking. In fact the Old Testament uses 'walk' more frequently in the sense of a lifestyle than it does of physical movement.

The language is apt. We can often tell a great deal about someone from how and where they walk. The way a person walks is one of the easiest ways to recognize them from a distance – 'I would recognize his walk a mile away' we sometimes say.

So it should be with Christian believers. How we conduct ourselves should make us easily recognised as those who belong to Christ. We walk in love; we walk in the light. Now, Paul adds two further details: (i) we are to take care how we walk, and (ii) we are to walk wisely.

CAREFUL NOW!

Look carefully is a good literal translation of Paul's words. He uses a verb (look, watch) and an adverb (carefully, accurately). His words imply that in living the Christian life we need *to think* about what we are doing, and to look to make sure we are on the right path, and not – like Christian in Bunyan's *Pilgrim's Progress* – wander off into by-path meadow. This requires wisdom – wisdom to see the dangers (temptation to sin, the weakness of the flesh, opposition from Satan); and wisdom to know how to respond in a godly and biblically instructed way.

How then do we walk? *Not as unwise but as wise.* In Scripture wisdom is always more than knowledge of factual information. It is possible to possess learning without wisdom. But wisdom is *savoir-faire*, being 'savvy' as we say colloquially. It is the ability to process knowledge into the practical ability to apply it to life situations and circumstances. It involves knowing how to achieve the best ends in the best way. Earlier Paul had given an illustration of this in the case of divine wisdom. God displays it in the way in which he has brought into being and preserved the church (3:10). He can point principalities and powers to it and say: 'Do you see my wisdom at work there? Be in awe of it and admire it, for I am God only wise'. The life of godliness, therefore, will reflect God's wisdom.

Paul mentions the hallmarks of the wise life:

USING TIME WELL

How do we respond to the question: What are the most valuable things in life to you – things too precious to waste? None of them is properly assessed until we realize the value of time and learn to use it rather than waste it.

Notice Paul's qualification here: *the days are evil.* While we have been delivered from 'the present evil age' (*Gal.* 1:4) we continue to live within its context and remain exposed to its influences. It is dominated, indeed obsessed with, the idea of living for the 'now' and turning a blind eye to eternity. Thus even the 'workaholic' – who apparently never wastes a minute – actually wastes every minute by living for self, for the short term, and for this world only. This – 'life under the sun' – as the author of Ecclesiastes describes it (*Ecc.* 1:3 etc.), is an empty striving after the wind. We reach out to take hold of what we have accomplished with our time, but since it lasts only for time, it crumbles in our hands.

But can we learn to be *making the best use of* this precious commodity? Paul uses the same verb of Christ redeeming us from the curse of the law (*Gal.* 3:13). His choice of vocabulary suggests that there is a price to be paid if we are to use time wisely. It needs to be bought back if we are to use it well in a fallen world. The concerns that dominate this 'present evil age' will exhaust it unless we save hard, purchase well, and use carefully. But with what coin can time be purchased for the glory of the Lord? The price is the self-discipline, which arises from a desire to glorify God in all things.

Paul adds an interesting comment. Time needs to be guarded because the *days are evil*. We, however, are more likely to think that they are harmless. But there is nothing harmless about an age that seems to regard leisure as an antidote for work, entertainment as an antidote to boredom. Rather than purchasing treasure we weaken our spiritual immune system as we breathe in the pollutants that ultimately destroy time's value.

What do you most instinctively think of doing when you have nothing to do? That is one of the tests. Are you a time-waster or a time-redeemer?

Perhaps you think Paul was guilty of exaggeration when he sought to motivate you by warning you that the days are evil? Perhaps that is why he now warns us against being *foolish* or, more literally, 'mindless'.

NOT MINDLESS, BUT UNDERSTANDING

The Christian – as we have just noted – is *a person who thinks*. That has already been implied in the idea of walking *in wisdom*. But how is it that by thinking we come to understand the will of God? Paul's own answer is revealed in his comments to Timothy: 'Think over what I say [which was, of course, inspired Scripture], for the Lord will give you understanding in everything' (*2 Tim.* 2:7). Illumination of the mind ordinarily comes by employing it in meditating on the divine wisdom revealed to us in Scripture and its application to all of life.

In this connection it is illuminating to notice how Paul's friend, the Gospel-writer Luke, describes our Lord's growth in wisdom into his teenage years (*Luke* 2:41–52).

Jesus viewed his life through the lenses of the so-called 'Servant Songs', which punctuate the second half of Isaiah. Perhaps the clearest statement about the way in which he grew to the full wisdom-capacity of his human nature is found in the third song:

> The Lord GOD has given me
> the tongue of those who are taught,
> that I may know how to sustain with a word
> him who is weary.
> Morning by morning he awakens;
> he awakens my ear
> to hear as those who are taught.
> The Lord GOD has opened my ear,
> and I was not rebellious;
> I turned not backwards.
>
> (*Isa.* 50:4–5)

It was by these means that our incarnate Lord grew in wisdom. He listened to the voice of God in the Scriptures, which he had committed to memory throughout his childhood years – which may have extended to the whole of the Old Testament.

It is obvious from the Gospels that Jesus thought deeply about God's Word and knew it. It was – as Psalm 119:103 taught him – like honey. And so the taste of Scripture lingered long after he had read the text, and was carried with him into every situation, helping him to see ways in which God's revealed will should be worked out into his life in personal obedience. As Jesus did this he grew not only in knowledge but also in wisdom – and in favour with God and man (*Luke* 2:52).

For Paul, the renewal of the mind is the key to the transformation of the life (cf. *Rom.* 12:1–2). God's regular guidance of his people is not a matter of 'voices' or extraordinary events. Rather, he leads us in the paths of righteousness – the *right* paths (*Psa.* 23:3). Ordinarily, he teaches us these paths in his Word directly, or by helping us to see the relevance of that Word to the providences of our lives. Understanding God's will comes from applying God's Word to our circumstances – always recognizing that the Lord may not yet have providentially unfolded all the circumstances that will enable us to move forwards with confidence. Wisdom often involves waiting – as Jesus did, realizing that his 'time' had not yet come (e.g. *John*. 7:6, 8).

Would anyone in need of wisdom think of asking you for it?

29

Filled with the Spirit

And do not get drunk with wine, for that is debauchery, but be filled with the Spirit, [19]addressing one another in psalms and hymns and spiritual songs, singing and making melody to the Lord with all your heart, [20]giving thanks always and for everything to God the Father in the name of our Lord Jesus Christ, [21]submitting to one another out of reverence for Christ. (Eph. 5:18–21)

We tend to think of conversion as a once-and-for-all event. But the New Testament teaches us that it is a life-long transformation with a once-and-for-all beginning. It involves repentance and faith, and we never leave repentance and faith behind; they are life long elements in the Christian life. As Martin Luther stated powerfully in the first of his famous *Ninety-Five Theses*: 'When our Lord Jesus Christ said "Repent" he meant that the whole of the Christian life should be repentance'.

The Christian life is an ongoing conversion, a putting away of the old, and a putting on of the new. Here Paul has been spelling out the contrast: wisdom replaces folly; redeeming the time replaces wasting the time. Now he adds a third contrast.

FILLED, BUT NOT DRUNK

One of the most obvious signs of being 'filled' with alcohol is an inability to walk properly and in a straight line – a loss of control. We call it being *drunk* (verse 18). Paul also describes it as *debauchery* – a giving way to uncontrolled passions which the sober person keeps in place. He may have in mind here aspects of pagan worship with which the Ephesians would have been all too familiar prior to their conversion.

Sometimes a new Christian will experience radical immediate deliverance from a habit of the old lifestyle and never looks back. But in other areas the fight and the struggle continue. For while we are once-and-for-all delivered from the dominion of sin, in many areas we may go through particularly severe 'withdrawal symptoms' from the ongoing presence of sin and the lingering influence of the addictions of our past life. A war may be decided by a critical single battle, yet troops find themselves facing 'mopping up operations'. These vary in intensity, but wounds inflicted in them are no less painful. So it is in the Christian life. To all of us Paul has the same counsel: Do not give way!

But this would never be Paul's last word on the matter. He teaches sanctification by displacement *and* replacement – not *drunk with wine* (which leads to *debauchery*) but rather *filled with the Spirit*.

BE 'BEING FILLED'

The Acts of the Apostles speaks on a number of occasions about people being 'filled with' or 'full of' the Spirit (*Acts* 2:4; 4:8, 31; 9:17; 13:9). Here, however, the form of the verb 'fill' is unique in the New Testament. It is

- present tense – an ongoing reality, not a once-for-all event
- imperative mood – it is a command which we are to obey, and
- passive voice – we do not fill ourselves, rather we receive the Spirit's fullness, we are filled with him. We are commanded: 'keep on being filled with the Spirit'

How does this unusual combination of ideas work – a *command* that seems to involve being *passive*?

Paul is carefully balancing two things: first that we are active in the experience of filling – God does not treat us as automatons; but, second, that this activity actually involves us being receptive (in that sense, 'passive') so that we are filled with the Spirit.

But how can this be? How can we *be filled with the Spirit*?

It is tempting here to fall back on our own experiences, or to turn to the stories told by others explaining 'how to' be filled with the

Spirit. But we are not cut adrift to find our own interpretation. For Paul's very similar teaching in Colossians 3:16–17 points us in the direction of his own understanding of what this involves.

HELP FROM COLOSSIANS

The letters to the Ephesians and the Colossians were written at the same time, carried by the same person (Tychicus) and have many similarities and parallels (*Eph.* 6:21; *Col.* 4:7).

Paul's statements in Ephesians 5:15, 18b–21 and in Colossians 3:16–17 stand in very close parallel to each other. They describe a similar series of effects in the Christian's life but attribute them to different causes. The consequences of being filled with the Spirit (*Eph.* 5:18) and the results of letting the Word of Christ indwell richly (*Col.* 3:16) run parallel to each other. The same fruit is produced by the influence of the Word of Christ as by the Spirit of Christ! Being *filled with the Spirit* and letting *the word of Christ dwell . . . richly* obviously amount to two ways of looking at the same thing.

Ephesians 5:15, 18b–21	*Colossians 3:16–17*
Be filled with the Spirit	Let the word of Christ dwell in you richly
. . . walk, not as unwise but as wise	in all wisdom
addressing one another	teaching and admonishing one another
in psalms and hymns and spiritual songs, singing and making melody to the Lord with all your heart,	singing psalms and hymns and spiritual songs, with thankfulness in your hearts to God
. . .and for everything . . . in the name of our Lord Jesus Christ	And whatever you do, in word or deed, do everything in the name of the Lord Jesus
giving thanks always to God the Father	giving thanks to God the Father through him

The way in which we obey the command to be filled with the Spirit is by responding to the Word of Christ – making room for its influence, giving our minds to its truth, our hearts to its teaching, and our wills to its obedience. To be under the influence of the Word is to place ourselves under the Lordship of the Spirit.

The man who is drunk cannot walk straight. His speech becomes slurred; he sings off key and out of tune and cannot remember the words; he becomes irritable when people try to help or reprimand; he will not have anyone else control his life – but he cannot control it himself.

The man or woman who is filled with the Spirit shows contrary graces: walking in wisdom; singing with melody in the heart, devoted to the Lordship of Christ, concerned for the needs of others, and thankful rather than irritable.

Three things here are worth special note.

(i) Paul teaches that the *melody* of our *heart* as we sing is directed to the Lord; but we direct our words not only to him but also to our fellow believers – we sing *addressing one another.*

This implies that our singing in worship has both a vertical and a horizontal direction. It also implies that it is legitimate in the praise of God to address the words we sing to others and even to ourselves. While too much contemporary praise may be over-saturated with references to ourselves, we should not lose sight of the fact that Paul learned this principle from the praise book of his childhood – the Psalms of David. In them we find a remarkably balanced division between words addressed to God, to others, and to the self.

In addition, Paul's words assume *that we will sing*! There is no dualism here (melody in the heart to the Lord, but no words on the lips!). Shame on me if I do not sing with heart and soul to the Lord and in order to bless my fellow worshippers with instruction and encouragement!

(ii) The second emphasis is on the simple grace of thankfulness. Paul had already noted the importance of this (verse 4). This is a world marked by deep ingratitude (*2 Tim.* 3:2). The church's corporate and enthusiastic thankfulness in everything makes it a light in the world, a city set on a hill that cannot be hidden. Alas if we are unthankful, if our worship is without energy! Alas if we do not see singing praises as also an opportunity to encourage one another! The loss is ours.

(iii) The third stress is that the fruit of the Spirit's fullness is the submissiveness of the believer: *submitting to one another out of reverence for Christ* (verse 21).

To submit here is, literally, 'to line up under' – as soldiers might do in placing themselves under their general. Paul will soon speak of the church's life as warfare against the powers of darkness. There is therefore an appropriateness in applying this military picture to the Christian life; especially when we remember the exhortation which opened this whole section – to strive to maintain the unity of our fellowship. Satan is always looking for ways to break it down and so mar the powerful witness to Christ that is present in a united fellowship (cf. *John.* 17:21–22).

Here, as in Philippians 2:1–11, Paul's remedy for disunity (and even for the potential of it) is humility – counting each other as more significant than ourselves (*Phil.* 2:3). That does not mean false modesty or a denial of the gifts the Lord has given us. It does, however, mean that the person filled with the Spirit will always be asking 'How can I serve my fellow believers?'

Our Saviour, Lord, and Model was 'full of the Holy Spirit' (*Luke* 4:1). He humbled himself and took the form of a servant (*Phil.* 2:7). Should we be prepared for anything less?

In the important section that follows, Paul will work out what this means in a variety of different contexts.

30

Wives and Their Husbands

> *Wives, submit to your own husbands, as to the Lord.* [23]*For the husband is the head of the wife even as Christ is the head of the church, his body, and is himself its Saviour.* [24]*Now as the church submits to Christ, so also wives should submit in everything to their husbands.* (Eph. 5:22–24)

Submission is the link between this section and the previous verse. But a further subsection of Paul's teaching begins here. How does it fit in to the overall structure of the letter?

The first words of the letter introduced us to the two spheres in which Christians live – the readers are simultaneously 'in Christ' and 'at Ephesus'.

In the opening three chapters Paul has, for all practical purposes, been expounding what it means for us to be 'in Christ'. On that foundation he has gone on to describe how the church and the individual believer are called to live in a way that 'fits' with the grace of God in the gospel.

The climax of this is the way in which believers not only 'fit in' with Christ but learn to 'fit in' with one another, willingly submitting to each other – not in the sense that there is no authority structure in the life of the church – but rather in personal relationships in the fellowship. Each member regards others as more important than himself or herself.

Now Paul takes the application of the gospel a stage further, into the three most basic relationships the Christian has in society: (i) marriage and home life; (ii) parents, children and family life; (iii) daily occupation and working life.

He begins with marriage, the health of which is essential both to the church and to society in general.

For Paul, Christ is at the heart of Christian marriage. Written deeply into its meaning and significance lies a *mystery* that is 'profound' (verse 32): Christ and the church.

Paul has been unfolding this mystery already – how all things will be brought into final submission to Christ the King. He has decisively defeated the powers of darkness, raised the spiritually dead, and brought reconciliation to believing Jews and Gentiles. In these different ways 'the mystery', whose final manifestation still awaits us, has already been revealed. Now Paul adds another sphere in which it is made known in the present time – in the lives of Christians whose marriages display the relationship between Christ and the church. It is in this context that he spells out the biblical recipe for a truly healthy marriage relationship. He speaks first of the responsibility of wives to their husbands and then vice-versa.

A SUBMISSIVE WIFE?

Paul's first exhortation *Wives, submit to your own husbands, as to the Lord* shocks our 'politically correct' culture. Yet widespread marital breakdown gives the lie to the contemporary self-confident rejection of the biblical teaching. Indeed, it reveals a deliberate blindness to God's pattern for human life – the pattern for which we were created and in which we discover the original purpose and destiny of marriage being fulfilled.

There is no verb *submit* in the text of verse 22. It is borrowed from the previous sentence about mutual submission in verse 21. Thus, a more literal translation would read: 'submitting to one another in reverence/fear of Christ . . . the wives to their own husbands in the Lord'. For that reason it is sometimes suggested that the overarching principle in this section is that of the *mutual* submission of believers. This mutual submission is then viewed as taking different forms, depending on whether one is a wife ('submit') or husband ('love'), child or father, slave or husband. In this interpretation, every exhortation Paul gives amounts to an expression of this mutual submission. Mutual submission is indeed our calling as Christians. But to regard that idea as the controlling element in interpreting what follows misreads the text – for three reasons:

(i) The same exhortation to wives appears in the parallel passage in Colossians 3:18. There the verb 'submit' is actually present in the statement but mutual submission is not mentioned in the broader context.

(ii) The model for the husband is Christ's *love* for the church not his *submission* to the church. While Christ is God's servant to the church, he never submits to it.

(iii) Ephesians 5:22–6:9 describe three contexts for relationships (marriage, family, household) in which submission is called for in one party but not in the other. These are forms of submission to God, not expressions of mutual submission to one another.

There is, of course, an appropriate mutual submission in marriage. The exhortation of 5:21 is to be obeyed by all Christians within the context of their mutual fellowship! But that is not the only aspect to the Christian life. Mutual submission no more obliterates the command in 5:22 than it rescinds the command of Hebrews 13:7 'Obey your leaders'!

Paul's point here is that in expressing the mystery of Christ, wives and husbands give expression to different dimensions of the relationship between the Lord and his people. In the case of the husband, as we shall see, his calling is to love, care for, and protect his wife as Christ does the church. But the wife's role in this domestic cameo of grace is to illustrate how the believer responds to Christ's love with deep and joyful submission.

In this context, Paul's counsel to the wife is focussed exclusively on her marriage relationship to her husband (the adjective *own* is emphatic here), not to men in general.

The calling is to submission. Our primary and absolute submission is to the Lord Jesus Christ. Here, in talking to believers, Paul urges wives to express that in their disposition towards and relationship with their husbands.

The reason for the submission is that *the husband is the head of the wife* (5:23). To be *head* in this context implies leadership (cf. 1:22 of Christ).

Contrary to this, some writers have claimed that the word 'head' here carries the connotation of 'source' rather than of 'authority'.

However, earlier, when he is speaking of Christ as 'head', he is thinking of his lordship, not of him as source of creation. He is head in the sense of king, not in the sense of source.

There is logic to what Paul says here about Christian marriage. The reason a Christian wife submits to her own husband is because of the God-given role of leadership and authority given to him. He is *head* of his wife not because woman was created out of Adam's rib ('source') but because God has constituted the relationship in this way, for his own purposes (cf. *1 Cor.* 11:3). It is not a matter of being bigger or stronger, but of the divine order and the divine mystery.

The scope of the submission is universal (verse 24: *in everything*). Conceivably there are situations where a wife should not obey her husband – if his leadership can be followed only by clear disobedience to God. (*Acts* 5:29 applies here too). But it is usually a danger sign when our *first* reaction to this exhortation is to find ways in which to restrict and limit it. Paul is encouraging glad, not reluctant, submission; wholeheartedness is the key. Indeed he takes this one stage further –

The manner of the submission is *as to the Lord* (verse 22; cf. *1 Pet.* 3:6). Here we come to the heart of the matter. The reason for the obedience is that in the marriage relationship a gospel drama is being portrayed in a unique way through a human relationship. The wife is expressing in her love for her husband how a believer responds to the Lord Jesus Christ. This is central to the mystery of Christ and his church, which is disclosed in Christian marriage.

What does this submission mean? It is not the subjection of an inferior human being to a superior one. God has created marriage so that husband and wife might be *one flesh* (verse 31). Rather it is the kind of submission that the hand gives to the head when it stretches out its fingers to help someone in need. Neither head nor hand can operate independently of the other; the hand does not direct the head; the hand's submission to the head involves service. So it is to be in a Christian marriage and home life.

Paul says that the wife's submission is *in everything*. That is, after all, how believers are to submit to Christ. Illustrating the mystery is, therefore, not only a tremendous privilege for husbands and wives; it is a challenge. Husbands and wives are sinners. The submission of a wife to her husband is not struggle-free.

Behind Paul's teaching here lies an important strand of biblical teaching that runs from creation through the fall into salvation:

i. Creation. Man was created first, and then woman. Man was created as the image and glory of God; woman as the glory of man (cf. *1 Cor.* 11:7–9), yet made to be one flesh with him (*Gen.* 2:23; cf. *Eph.* 5:29). There is equality of being, even a union between two people. But this is set within two different roles.

ii. Fall. In the original creation it would have been 'natural' for Eve to fulfil her unique role as helper to Adam. It was this that the serpent overturned. He tried to confuse her about what God had actually said (*Gen.* 3:1ff). That was tantamount to denying what Adam her husband had told her. Eve listened to the voice of the serpent rather than the voice of her husband (and thus rather than to the voice of God). Adam appears to have been present but remained silent. He listened to the voice of his wife (*Gen.* 3:17) and thus also sinned by not listening to the voice of God.

The result of this is expressed in the words God spoke to Eve: 'Your desire shall be for [or against] your husband, and [or but] he shall rule over you' (*Gen.* 3:16b). The form of this statement suggests that the 'desire' in view is Eve's desire to master Adam. The same language reappears in Genesis 4:7 with this nuance. Eve's decision of the moment became the habit of a lifetime.

iii. Salvation. In Christ the fall is reversed. He obeyed where Adam failed; he took the divine judgment Adam deserved. The result is that, through the Spirit, he begins to restore and remake what was fractured and twisted at the fall. This is what is being worked out and exhibited in the relationship of a wife to her husband.

Marriage is not a recipe for the subjugation of a woman, but a blueprint for her true freedom in a healthy, loving relationship with her husband. Best of all, it means that in our marriage and home life the wonder, power, beauty, holiness and transformation of the gospel can be seen – not only by the rest of the family, but also by those who are not yet believers.

It is marvellous that the Lord has so constituted marriage that a Christian wife can illustrate the life of faith by her response to her husband. Such a wife expresses the evangelistic power of married love.

But by the same token we have the ability to mask the truth of the gospel by our resistance to the patterns of God's Word. Therein lies the challenge to a Christian wife.

31

Husbands and Their Wives

Husbands, love your wives, as Christ loved the church and gave himself up for her, [26]that he might sanctify her, having cleansed her by the washing of water with the word, [27]so that he might present the church to himself in splendour, without spot or wrinkle or any such thing, that she might be holy and without blemish. [28]In the same way husbands should love their wives as their own bodies. He who loves his wife loves himself. [29]For no one ever hated his own flesh, but nourishes and cherishes it, just as Christ does the church, [30]because we are members of his body. [31]'Therefore a man shall leave his father and mother and hold fast to his wife, and the two shall become one flesh.' [32]This mystery is profound, and I am saying that it refers to Christ and the church. [33]However, let each one of you love his wife as himself, and let the wife see that she respects her husband. (Eph. 5:25–33)

Did God give the wife or the husband the more demanding role in marriage? It seems to be assumed automatically today that Paul demanded that wives play the more difficult role.

But now these words are set in an altogether different light. Husbands are to love their wives as Christ loved the church! What Christian would claim that the believer has a more difficult role than the Saviour? Christ is the one called by his Father to sacrifice himself in love for us; we are the ones called to submit to him. Which is the greater demand?

The model for and the measure of a husband's love is to be – Jesus Christ. If there were any suspicion that Paul was placing too heavy a burden on wives this dissolves it immediately.

THE COVENANT OF LOVE

Further qualifications of this love are given. The love in view is sacrificial and cross-shaped. It will not stop short at absorbing pain and even dying for the loved one. It is also a love that has sanctification as its goal. Just as Christ died to *sanctify* the church (verse 26), cleansing it from all impurities, so the sacrificial love of a husband has in view the personal growth and spiritual beauty of his wife (cf. *1 Pet.* 3:3–6).

The background to this concept lies, of course, in the Old Testament's understanding of Yahweh's relationship with his people as a marriage covenant. This love story is poignantly described in Ezekiel 16. Finding Israel abandoned and filthy, the Lord had compassion on her and gave her life. He nourished her and entered into a marriage-bond with her. He not only provided for her needs but also lavished blessings on her. Yet Israel proved to be a faithless wife, indeed a harlot.

Paul has earlier described how God has entered into a new covenant in Christ; he has forged a bond with believing Jew and Gentile to be the bride for his Son. He has made us his own *by the washing of water with the word.* The words echo those of Jesus to Nicodemus: only those born of water and the Spirit see and enter the kingdom of God. That supernatural birth cleanses us. It ordinarily takes place within the context of the proclamation of the gospel ('the word' cf. *James* 1:18*; 1 Pet.* 1:23).

The gospel itself is thus a manual for husbands, training them how to love their wives. This is their challenge: they do not exist for themselves; a husband must commit himself to blessing his wife. He must live, and if necessary, die for her.

Paul drives this point home by underlining the practical implications of his biblical theology of marriage. There is a sense in which it would be unnatural for a husband *not* to love his wife in this way. For, according to the teaching of Genesis 2:23–24, he has become *one flesh* with his wife (verse 31). If someone hates his own flesh we regard him as unbalanced, perhaps psychotic. For a husband not to love his wife – who has become one flesh with him – is not only to be a poor husband, it is to be a dysfunctional Christian!

The *mystery* here is *profound* (verse 32), hidden into the heart of the marriage bond. This relationship points to another, greater, more fundamental and lasting relationship: the marriage between Christ and the church.

God has built into the order of creation a relationship which – yes, with all its own mysteries – provides a clue to the Ultimate Relationship, the experience of being a couple in a marriage relationship that points to the Ultimate Couple – Christ and his Bride, the church. This marriage 'made in heaven', but forged on earth, is destined to last for all eternity. And every Christian marriage is called to reflect and manifest it. Glorious mystery indeed!

PRACTICAL IMPLICATIONS

These verses as a whole contain exalted teaching. But like all biblical teaching it has very practical implications and is 'profitable for . . . reproof, for correction, and for training in righteousness, that the man of God may be competent, equipped for every good work' (*2 Tim.* 3:16–17).

For one thing, Paul gives us this teaching at length because he realized that from the beginning marriage has been attacked by Satan because it represents the culmination of God's gifts, a companionship that made man's environment 'very good' (*Gen.* 1:31).

Satan hated that. He did all he could to destroy it. And so he brought division between the woman and the man. No longer is Eve submissive; no longer does Adam love and protect her with a love-unto-death. Genesis 3 soon portrays them at each other's throats as the serpent slinks away into the shadows.

If this was true in the Garden, it remains true today. Marriage is under attack. In the midst of the encroaching darkness, married Christians need to recognize that their relationships too will be under attack. But the darkness also provides an opportunity for light to shine in it and to expose it for what it really is. When a Christian husband loves his wife on the model of the love of Christ for the church, and a wife submits to her husband in the happy acquiescence that expresses the believer's submission to Christ – then light shines, fills the home, and spills out into the neighbourhood.

Furthermore, Paul's teaching here gives guidance for family life. Marriage brings a new 'one-flesh' unit into being. Hence, it involves a leaving the old and the beginning of something new (verse 31).

There is a readjustment of the former family structures. All members of the family need to remember that!

A Christian marriage thus has great evangelistic power in and beyond the home. Among other married couples a Christian marriage can witness to the grace of Christ on which it is based. Christ's love for us is displayed through the husband's love for his wife, our submission to him in faith through the wife's loving submission to her husband. Children should be able to see the gospel in their parents' lifestyle. By God's grace the Christ-like love and Christ-centred devotion seen in their parents will encourage them to trust and obey him as Saviour and Lord.

All this leads to a final application – not an insignificant one, since Paul will now turn to address the next generation in the church. Understanding and appreciating this teaching enables us to prepare for marriage and to sense whether someone to whom we are naturally attracted would be a suitable life partner.

The answer to these questions might help to settle the matter – permanently:

- Am I prepared to have, and do I wish this man to be my head? Would it be for my long-term blessing, and for the advance of Christ's kingdom, to submit to him?
- Do I love this woman with a desire to see her sanctified and blessed, and would I do anything to care for and protect her?

Here is marriage guidance counsel that can be read in a matter of minutes. But it takes a lifetime of faithfulness and love to work it out.

32

Children and Parents

> *Children, obey your parents in the Lord, for this is right.* [2] *'Honour your father and mother' (this is the first commandment with a promise),* [3] *'that it may go well with you and that you may live long in the land.'* [4] *Fathers, do not provoke your children to anger, but bring them up in the discipline and instruction of the Lord.* (Eph. 6:1–4)

The transformation brought about by the gospel affects every area of life. The old gives way to the new. Paul is now addressing three basic structures in our lives in which this comes to expression: husbands and wives in their marriage and home; parents and children and the rearing of a family; masters and slaves in the workaday world. The gospel of grace applies to each area. In fact, there is no situation in which it cannot work!

But how do we 'walk in a manner worthy of the calling' (4:1) within the context of family life? Biblical instruction here is as important today as it was in the first century. Western societies that sowed the wind in their rejection of biblical teaching are beginning to reap the whirlwind in the disintegration of family life.

For that reason the teaching of this paragraph is as profoundly counter-cultural as the verses that preceded it. Sadly, in many ways it is also counter-church-cultural. For Paul seems to expect that children will be present in the Christian assembly to hear his letter read, as they would hear the 'other Scriptures' (*2 Pet.* 3:16). Paul assumed that there would be children in the assembly when his letter was read. Did he grasp something we have missed? When some churches complain that they are 'losing the young people' from worship the truth is that they have never actually been present at it. Of course, there may be more to it than this; much more. But if we send a subliminal message to our children 'You do not belong here; you would not enjoy it' we say something about ourselves (if worship were important to us we would do everything to encourage our children to share that perspective!). We also say something to the children. It should not surprise us if they hear what our actions say as well as our words. How different Paul's view – and our Lord's view – of children!

The pattern of Paul's teaching here resembles the earlier section on husbands and wives: it begins by addressing those who are to submit (here *obey*) and then turns to describe the responsibilities of those to whom that submission is made.

RELATIONSHIPS WITH PARENTS

Paul pastors the younger members of the church in a gospel-centred, grace orientated, spiritually wise manner. He spells out their obligation, enhances it with a qualification, and encourages them with an all-important motivation.

Whether we are children, or parents, or pastors, or simply friends, it is important to grasp Paul's method as well as the substance of his message: never express the obligation to obedience without also stressing the motivation of grace. The whole letter is built on such a pattern; all of its individual parts express it in miniature. It cannot be over-stressed how important it is that we communicate this to our children.

OBLIGATION

Children are to *obey* their *parents*. Paul's verb expresses this in a picturesque way. Its root meaning is 'to hear under' – to listen as someone who places himself or herself 'under', not 'over' what is being said.

This is reminiscent of Luke's description of Jesus. As a youngster he engaged with God's Word in his discussions with the teachers in the Temple (they were amazed at both his understanding of the Scriptures and his answers to their questions of him, *Luke* 2:46–47). He gently, but firmly, reminded his parents of his relationship to the Father (*Luke* 2:49, cf. *Psa*. 27:4, 8). He 'was submissive to them'

(*Luke* 2:51). At the age of twelve he already had more understanding than his elders (*Psa.* 119:100); but he did not therefore despise their role or that of his parents in his life. He had more wisdom than Mary and Joseph, yet he was submissive to them – even although they had been in error.

Should we, as children, do less than our Lord did?

If you are young you may feel there is very little you can do to serve the Lord. Here is a special word for you. Your loving obedience to your parents may be the very thing that makes other families wonder 'What has his or her family got that we don't have? Their relationships with each other seem so different from ours.'

In a day when many families are alienated from each other, where there is sharp tension, where parents are often paralysed in relationships with their children – terrified not only to say 'no' to them but to say anything to them – what a wonderful witness a Christian young person can be to others – like a Stephen to a Saul of Tarsus who, strive as he might, cannot emulate the grace he sees!

QUALIFICATION

Paul adds a qualification. Children are to be obedient *in the Lord*. Some parents command their children to do things that are absolutely contrary to the will of God. But Paul is not thinking about that difficult situation here. He is addressing Christian parents and their children. The words *in the Lord* point up the context of their relationship. Everything is to be seen within the context of our loving fellowship together with the Lord Jesus Christ. In that fellowship we have different roles. That of children is to learn to obey the heavenly Father by obeying their earthly fathers. God trains us to respond to his Fatherhood (which we cannot see) by responding to earthly fatherhood (which we can see!). He thinks of everything as he trains us to serve him in the future!

MOTIVATION

What Paul has already said is motivation enough. But he now spells out the gospel motives that encourage us to live in this way.

It is the *right* way to live (*for this is right* verse 1). Children who obey their parents are living the way God intended. Any other way eventually breaks the family – as many passages in the Bible, including the Old Testament child-training manual, the Book of Proverbs, underline. So when a youngster is 'filled with the Spirit' as the young Lord Jesus surely was, it comes to expression in obedience to the law of God: 'Honour your father and mother' (*Exod.* 20:12; *Deut.* 5:16).

It is the way to inherit the promise. The fifth commandment is the *first* to spell out a specific *promise* of life for those who obey it: 'that it may go well with you and that you may live long in the land'. This must never be isolated from other promises in Scripture (e.g. that the Lord will also be with us in times when things do not seem to go well). In essence it is saying: live in faithfulness to God's covenant in your relationship to your parents and you will discover that the promises of the Lord's blessing are true.

It is worth noting three further details here.

i. The fifth commandment involves the broader idea of 'honour' not only the narrower idea of 'obedience'. At every stage of life – childhood, teenage years, adulthood, even old age – we should honour our parents. The specific outworking of that will develop in relationship to the varying circumstances and stages of life. Paul has already indicated that marriage changes the structure of our relationships: we leave our parents and hold fast to our spouse (verse 31). A new primary relationship is established. The way in which we honour our parents will take account of that. But when we are young children, honour is first of all expressed in obedience.

ii. Paul speaks about the fifth commandment as *the first commandment with a promise* (6:2). In fact it is the *only one* of the commandments with a promise! Does Paul mean that for children it is the *first* commandment, and that there is a very special promise attached to it to encourage children to obey it? It is as if the Lord were saying to children in homes marked by faith: 'Love, trust, and obey your father and mother. In obeying this command you will soon learn what all the other commandments mean.'

iii. Paul refers to *the commandment* in a way that implies that this specific commandment (and by implication the Decalogue as a whole) is still applicable to the gospel lifestyle. The reason is not far to seek: children are to obey the fifth commandment because *this is right* (6:1). The same is true of the substance of the other commandments. God has given them to us because they describe the way life is meant to be lived.

At Sinai these commandments were given with a special shape applicable to their immediate context. But Paul assumes and implies the substance of all Ten Commandments remains relevant for contemporary Christians because they were rooted in God's creation of man as his image. Paul did not encourage children to be obedient to their parents because they lived in a dominantly patriarchal and hierarchical society. He encouraged it because it is *right*. It is as simple as that – for this and for all of the commandments!

The lifelong lesson is surely obvious: look for ways to honour your father and mother, no matter what your stage of life! Find them as soon as you can. It may yet transform family relationships and things will indeed *go well with you*!

33

Parents and Children

Fathers, do not provoke your children to anger, but bring them up in the discipline and instruction of the Lord. (Eph. 6:4)

Paul's teaching on our basic relationships in life is demanding as well as instructive. That may be why he begins with counsel for those whose responsibility it is to express their love for Christ in submissiveness to another.

There may be more than one reason for this order. At first sight we might think that it gets the more difficult and less palatable exhortation 'out of the way'; it goes against the grain of our independent hearts to submit to anyone!

But a second glance suggests that this may not be the case. The command to the husband to show Christ-like, self-denying, life-laying-down, love for his wife is even more demanding than the summons to the wife to submit to her own husband.

When we are children we are likely to think that the child has the harder lot! Then we become parents . . . and then realize the challenge that faced our own father! A father's task is in many ways more complex and more challenging – it is the task with the greater responsibilities, and it is long term!

Paul's words (i) are addressed to *fathers*; (ii) give a negative warning; and (iii) provide positive directives.

FATHERS

Since children are to obey their 'parents' (6:1) why does Paul here address only *fathers*? A father possessed enormous power over his children in Paul's world. In fact the Latin language had an expression for it – 'father-power'! A father could make or break his children.

The same is still true, if in less formal ways. Paul's concern here is to transform fatherhood, we might even say to 'gospel' it. Like every aspect of sanctification, being a Christian father involves no longer living under the dominion of self but for the Lord Jesus (*2 Cor.* 5:15). There is a negative refusal of the pattern of the old life and a positive embracing of the graces of the new life – always both together.

How does this work out in fatherhood?

A FATHER'S RESTRAINT

Fathers, do not provoke your children to anger (verse 4). In the parallel passage in Colossians Paul explains one reason: this is the high road that leads to the discouragement of our children (cf. *Col. 3:21*). It demeans and destroys them.

There is a divinely given wisdom in everything Paul says here. It is, of course, a father's responsibility to teach his children God's way (verse 4b spells this out). But while Paul urges children to obey, he also sees a danger.

Some fathers try to subordinate their children to their own authority and the necessity of obeying it in such a way that they obscure rather than express the gracious authority of God. The duties of children are thus severed from a context of love, the relationship with the father is divorced from faith – and the effect is to *provoke to anger*.

The child's responsibility is not Paul's concern for the moment. He is stressing that a father does not have the right to 'lord it' over his children. A domineering spirit is not a divine instrument. Commandment is always given by God in the context of grace; grace with a view to obedience – these are the ways in which the Lord gives blessing. Fathers should imitate the Father in this regard.

Paul's words provide a valuable litmus test for a father: What specific sins in me might provoke my children to anger? Indifference to them would be one. Having a favourite would be another. These are matters of the heart, of the inner disposition; they emerge in all kinds of subtle ways. Children not only hear the words we say, they breathe in the disposition, the attitudes, the preferences and prejudices, the likes and dislikes that we breathe out. They see when we do not treat them as individuals.

Treating our children 'all the same' means treating each of them as uniquely created in the image of God. Zealous Christians are sometimes convinced that it is possible to 'clone' children according to a one-size-fits-all pattern they have seen described in a book (perhaps even a Christian book!) on child-rearing. Beware! Scripture gives us wonderful principles (the entire Book of Proverbs, for example); but it never releases us from the responsibility to learn how to apply these principles to individual and very different flesh-and-blood children! That task summons us to trust in God's covenant promises (our own flesh is incapable of accomplishing the task) and to live by faith.

Paul's words, then, warn us of the danger of law without grace. This almost inevitably leads to the child-frustration of which Paul speaks. What, then, positively are we to do?

THE FATHER'S NURTURE

Fathers are to set their hearts on learning to *bring up* their children *in the discipline and instruction of the Lord* (6:4). Paul's choice of words here is illuminating.

Bring up is the verb 'nourish' which Paul had earlier used of the care a person has for his own body, of the devotion of Christ to the church, and therefore of the practical love a husband should have for his wife (5:29).

The model is already set before the father in the grace of Christ towards him. As part of the church he has been loved and nourished by Christ the Bridegroom. In addition, the husband should have grown in the practice of this grace over his years of fellowship with his wife (5:25)! His attitude to his children is an overflow of these two relationships.

There is a beautiful harmony and integrity running right through the Christian life. We have been the recipients of great tenderness at the hands of Christ. Husbands have been called to show great tenderness to their wives. They are now called as fathers to express this tenderness to their children.

Discipline (verse 4) is, literally, 'child-training'. Perhaps in the many hours spent in the lecture hall of Tyrannus, Paul had worked his way through much of the biblical teaching on parenting. If so, he would have built deep foundations for these young Christians in such passages as Deuteronomy 6 and 11, Proverbs 1–8, and Psalm 119. The training in view in these passages was profound, biblical, spiritual, and eminently practical. The model father of the Old Testament took the deepest interest in his children. By word and example he taught them wise principles to enable them to respond to the wide variety of situations in life. In particular, he taught them how to deal with sin and temptation.

Instruction translates a term Paul uses in one form or another in a number of places. Literally it means 'to place in the mind'. Sometimes it carries the idea of admonition, instruction with a view to transformed behaviour. It was a hallmark of Paul's own ministry (*Col.* 1:28) and is to be a characteristic of the life and worship of the church (*Col.* 3:16).

In the modern world, bringing up children has often, by default, become the task of mothers. But gratitude for the role played by mothers does not absolve fathers from their responsibility. They are called to be the means by which God builds into children the internal laws of grace and holiness that give drive and direction to the Christian life.

Paul's counsel is for the long haul. It cannot be accomplished in one day, one week, one month, one year, even one decade. Fathers must learn that their calling is to invest in the long term – and not to lose sight of that in the light of short-term gains. It is all too easy to trust in the flesh. The boasts of one Christmas family letter may become the griefs of later ones.

Our devotion to the disciplines of the Lord in our own lives is tested within the context of the family. There are many mysteries and imponderables in child-rearing; our children are different and separate individuals. Parents are only instruments of the Lord. At the end of the day, there are many privileges in belonging to a Christian family. But the flesh profits nothing; only the Spirit gives life. So we learn to entrust our children to the Lord and to ask for his grace to abound to them.

Underlying all this teaching is an important principle. The spiritual nourishment of children lies with their parents. Theirs is the first responsibility. The church community may help for a few hours each week. But parents have their children seven days in the week, fifty-two weeks in the year, often for seventeen years or more of their lives. Sometimes that seems a long time. But one day it will seem to have been very short. Family life is not a video we can rewind in order to start again. We are given one opportunity, extended over time. We need to use it well.

That we can do only with the help of the Best and Wisest Father.

34

Slaves and Masters

> *Slaves, obey your earthly masters with fear and trembling, with a sincere heart, as you would Christ, [6]not by the way of eye-service, as people-pleasers, but as servants of Christ, doing the will of God from the heart, [7]rendering service with a good will as to the Lord and not to man, [8]knowing that whatever good anyone does, this he will receive back from the Lord, whether he is a slave or free. [9]Masters, do the same to them, and stop your threatening, knowing that he who is both their Master and yours is in heaven, and that there is no partiality with him.* (Eph. 6:5–9)

The Roman Empire of the first century was a world of slavery on the grand scale. A century before Paul sent his letter to Ephesus, Julius Caesar reportedly shipped back to Rome somewhere in the region of a million slaves. They made up anywhere between twenty and thirty-five percent of the population. Without them the Empire could never have functioned as it did.

In this context slaves fulfilled a wide variety of roles, from the menial through the mundane, to the highest activities. Some of them became learned men who served in skilled capacities in education and civil service; some were able to accumulate considerable wealth or influence. Felix, for example, the Roman governor of Judea, before whom Paul appeared (*Acts* 23:23ff.), was once a slave but had managed to establish his freedom and gain political position. In that sense many Roman slaves were not economically and socially degraded as in some cultures. Others, as we know, were humiliated and harshly, sometimes brutally treated.

The abolition of slavery was far from the mind of the apostle Paul. In any case, he was utterly powerless to bring it about and it would have been futile for him to attempt it. Furthermore, Paul operated under the deep conviction that social and personal conditions were not the primary issue in life – fellowship with God, freedom from sin, transformation into Christ-likeness, and the advance of the kingdom of God – these were his central concerns. The gospel works anywhere. Nothing can hinder it, whether physical imprisonment (which Paul was at that very moment experiencing 3:1; 4:1), or the social chains of slavery (which undoubtedly some of his hearers knew at first hand). In our own time the gospel has advanced in many countries in the world in the face of violent opposition and persecution. Nothing, ultimately, can thwart the power of the gospel.

Here, then, we have apostolic teaching on how the gospel of grace functions in a social order we find intolerable. But the principles Paul enunciates are also applicable today to the social order with which we are familiar. We are not slaves. We have not been sold to a master. Yet we have 'sold' forty or so hours in the week, in many cases, to a 'master'. We do this under carefully controlled conditions (we can withdraw our labour, we have organized support groups; we do not fear physical reprisals). Yet there are lessons here about attitudes and the use of time that we can apply to our own workaday situation.

DIFFERENT ATTITUDE

Paul continues the general teaching of this section of the letter (the Christian is different – a new man – and therefore behaves differently). He repeats the specific note he has struck throughout this subsection on basic relationships (the Christian is characterized by a spirit of appropriate submission because he or she has submitted to Jesus Christ). The basic disposition of a believer is different from that of the unbeliever, and his or her style of living is different too. Paul therefore lists several marks of the *Christian* slave.

Slaves are to *obey* their *masters*, and to do so with *fear and trembling* (verse 5). The word *fear* (*phobos*, cf. our word 'phobia', a fear of something) can mean anything from loving reverence to real terror. In this context the meaning is nearer the former than the latter. Paul has used it in this sense in 5:21 (we are to submit to one another in reverence/fear/honour/respect of Christ) and 5:33 (where he says that the wife reverences/fears/honours/respects her husband).

Here however Paul takes this a stage further. He uses the phrase *fear and trembling*. Elsewhere he taught that this disposition is to characterize the Christian in general; we are to work out our salvation with 'fear and trembling' (*Phil.* 2:12). There it refers to the Christian's disposition towards the Lord. The same expression is used to describe the way the Corinthians received Titus (*2 Cor.* 7:15). In both instances it describes a loyalty whose nervousness lies in the thought that a loved one might be let down. Paul is calling for the same godly disposition here, as he adds *with a sincere heart, as you would Christ*. It is in the relation of the believer to his or her master that expression is given to the relationship with heaven that lies behind it.

All this is qualified by the key words *as you would Christ*. The disposition of the converted slave towards his master is explained only by his disposition towards his true Master. For that, rather than the mere human context, is his incentive to live out the new life of the gospel.

Because of this, the believing slave – and Paul assumes that both slaves and masters would be sitting in the assembly – works wholeheartedly for his earthly master. Just as thankfulness motivates obedience to Christ it also spills over into quality service – out of love and reverence for him.

This same spirit is transferable to the workplace in the contemporary world, transforming our daily work and simultaneously enhancing our witness to Christ.

DIFFERENT MOTIVE

The gospel has a subversive character. The earthly master who is not a believer cannot understand why the Christian slave is so responsive, so gracious, so diligent. Obedience to the master is not *by way of eye-service, as people-pleasers* (verse 6). Indeed, it does not have the earthly master, ultimately, in view. It is always an expression of obedience to Christ, the True and Best Master whose service is perfect freedom. The slave's good will to his master is an expression of his love for his Lord. Thus a slave could enjoy an inner freedom from the master who regarded himself as the centre of the universe

– too short sighted to notice that his Christian slave was looking far beyond *earthly masters* to a heavenly one and was serving him (verse 8)!

When we learn to do things for Christ we are set free from earthly servility and find joy and pleasure in our labours. We know that they can never be in vain in the Lord (*1 Cor.* 15:58). Moreover, since we do them for his pleasure, they bring him pleasure – and this in turn is our greatest pleasure.

DIFFERENT PERSPECTIVE

Paul now turns (verse 9) to Christians who were slave owners. Why does he not tell them to free their slaves? Probably many Christians did exactly that. But in effect that would have had no immediate impact on the practice of slavery. Did Paul realize that God has his time and place for everything, and understand that sometimes more is accomplished through deprivation than through liberty? It is the suffering of believers rather than their prosperity that God characteristically uses to advance his kingdom and build the church.

But the Christian master had then (and has now) important responsibilities. As owner and/or employer the gospel must transform his perspective. He is called to serve Christ, to be a master who expresses in practical ways what it means to be a new man in Christ. Thus masters are to *do the same to them* [i.e. their slaves]. That is, despite very different social spheres both master and slave live out the same kingdom principles in all of their relationships.

As a result, in sharp contrast to many ungodly slave owners, the Christian master does not threaten (the *ESV* translation, *stop your threatening* suggests that some Christian masters still needed to work this principle through, as doubtless some Christian fathers needed the words 'do not provoke your children . . . ' 6:4). Grace transforms threats into encouragements. Imagine what a surprise it must have been to slaves whose master was converted when the spirit of the entire household was transformed!

The Christian master does not show *partiality* (verse 9). Like his Master he will begin to demonstrate grace without qualifications. The master realizes that he is not lord. Christ alone is, and he is Lord of both slave and master. Before him both are equal.

This is a unique view of life. One lesson it teaches us is how muddleheaded it is to regard work and witness as two different realities for the Christian. We witness in the work we do, by the way we do it – as if we were doing it to the Lord Christ. If we are his, we are.

Have you learned that the gospel can work anywhere, under any circumstances? The grass always seems greener somewhere else! The gospel's power is not dependent on favourable human situations or sympathetic people but on the power of God, the grace of Christ, and the presence of the Holy Spirit. This made first-century slaves free men and women in Christ long before the abolition of slavery.

If the gospel of Jesus Christ can work under those circumstances, it can surely work where you spend forty hours or more each week.

35

Life Is a Battle

Finally, be strong in the Lord and in the strength of his might. [11]Put on the whole armour of God, that you may be able to stand against the schemes of the devil. [12]For we do not wrestle against flesh and blood, but against the rulers, against the authorities, against the cosmic powers over this present darkness, against the spiritual forces of evil in the heavenly places. (Eph. 6:10–12)

The powers of darkness opposed God's kingdom; spiritual death ruled the Ephesians; deep seated alienation existed between Jew and Gentile. But now, in Christ, these obstacles had been dealt death blows. Already in the lives of individuals and whole churches the dawning of the new age had come.

At the beginning of this magnificent letter Paul had described Christians as being 'in Christ' even while they were still 'at Ephesus'. More than that, they had already begun to taste and enjoy the spiritual blessings of the new age, 'in the heavenly places' (1:3).

Now, as Paul returns to talk about life in those *heavenly places* (verse 12), he introduces a surprising turn of events. This realm where spiritual blessings are received is also the location of an ongoing spiritual battle. While Christ has delivered the deathblow to the powers of darkness, they are not yet finally destroyed. To be raised from spiritual death into spiritual life by Christ the King means that we are no longer the followers (or prisoners) of the prince of the power of the air (2:2). We are now 'the opposition'. But precisely as such we have become the object of all his recriminating and destructive forces. Consequently, the final proof that we have been raised up to sit with Christ in the heavenly places and now walk in a way that is worthy of him is: we keep our feet and are able to remain standing in the battle against the Evil One.

Early in the Christian life we might think that *to stand* (verse 11) in this spiritual warfare is a relatively insignificant achievement. But the more we read the New Testament, and the longer we experience the pressure of spiritual warfare, the more clearly we will see that to remain standing – after all the heat of the battle – is the result of a work of supernatural grace in us. This is why Paul reiterates the idea (verses 11, 13 twice, 14).

Three issues are common to battles of every kind:

(i) What is the context and nature of the battle?
(ii) Who is the enemy and what is his strength?
(iii) What are our resources for defence and victory?

THE BATTLE GROUND

i. This battle is fought *in the heavenly realms*, the sphere into which we have been brought through our election and union to Christ (cf. 1:3; 2:6; 3:10). To live in this atmosphere is to be brought into the centre of a conflict zone. This is the context in which the whole Bible, from Genesis 3:15 onwards is set – the ongoing warfare between the Lord and the serpent (grown into the size of a dragon by the end of the Scriptures, *Rev.* 12:9).

This is exactly what our Lord promised: 'I will build my church and the gates of hell shall not prevail against it' (*Matt.* 16:18). To become a citizen in this kingdom is to be caught up in a cosmic conflict where the issues are of eternal moment. This is why Peter warns us of the devouring lionesque desires of the Evil One (*1 Pet.* 5:8). He needs to be detected and resisted.

ii. But far from being ethereal and mystical the regular context of the battle is *in the ordinary routines of daily life*. It is at Ephesus (cf. 1:1 and 3) the conflict is joined. Wherever grace brings advance and victory, attacks will come. It is in the ordinary progress of sanctification that the Devil seeks to defeat us; it is in daily routines that we need to make sure he gains no foothold (cf. 4:27). Mundane life, not just mountaintop experience, is the sphere in which Satan appears. We need to be conscious of his stratagems.

This is brought out remarkably in the context of Ephesians 6:10ff. – for Paul has just been discussing marriage, family life, and everyday employment. This was where Satan first successfully attacked. It was not when Adam and Eve were attempting extraordinary spiritual work for God, but when everything seemed mundane, that Satan tracked them down and tripped them up. In fact, their marriage, which was the best of all God's basic provisions for them, became the strongest instrument Satan could use to set them at odds against God and each other (cf. *Gen.* 3:1ff.). It is in marriage, parent-child relations, and in the daily working world that we need to recognize we are not dealing merely with flesh and blood but with *rulers . . . authorities . . . cosmic forces . . . spiritual forces of evil* (6:10).

iii. There is a further dimension to the way Satan musters his forces. He plans to strike *in the evil day*. What does this mean? Our Lord experienced such a day. The night of his betrayal was the hour of the power of darkness (*Luke* 22:53). He felt the full force of Satan's attack. Now came the greatest pressure to turn away from the cross. Since Satan could not destroy him by the temptation to go another way than to the cross, now he would seek to dominate the event itself, inciting one apostle to betray and another to deny, while scattering the rest.

Earlier in our Lord's ministry Satan sought to keep him from the way of the cross. Later, he seems to have been in a frenzy of activity in order to bring him to the cross in such a way that he might destroy Jesus' relationship with the Father.

By *the evil day* Paul may mean a still-future day when the conflict between the kingdoms of darkness and light will reach a consummation. But even if this is so, that day is already prefigured in our lives from time to time.

Unlike our Lord (*John.* 14:30), a 'landing place' for Satan remains in us. We are still sinners; there is still a 'Trojan Horse' of sin within us, which Satan seeks to use to make his dark strategies and snares effective. Sometimes we have opportunities to sin but lack any inner compulsion to pursue them; at other times we experience an inner compulsion but opportunity is lacking or we are providentially protected from taking it. But when temptation, desire, and opportunity coincide, the 'evil day' has come. So it was for David (*2 Sam.* 11:1ff.); so it may be for us. Then it is all we can do *to stand*. Indeed to remain standing is a great fruit of grace in us.

iv. But there is yet a further aspect to this. The battle is to be waged by us *in the Lord*. We cannot rely on our own resources to defeat Satan. He has experience stretching back to the Garden of Eden (*Gen.* 3:1ff.) and beyond (*Rev.* 12:4 possibly refers to his leading of a pre-fall rebellion in the heavenly world).

In general Paul's words point us back to the blessings and resources that have become ours in Christ as the one who has conquered all his and our enemies (cf. 1:15–23). Now, in Ephesians 6, as we shall see, Paul spells out in detail how to benefit from being *in the Lord* by wearing the *armour* he provides.

But before turning to consider this armour it is important to recognize why it needs to be so effective and why it is so urgent that we wear it.

THE CHARACTER OF THE ENEMY

One of the most important elements in warfare is reconnaissance – learning as much as possible about the enemy before we meet him. Military intelligence is always a prerequisite to victory.

When we first encounter Satan in Genesis 3 he seems to have done his reconnaissance already, almost without Eve (and Adam) realizing what was happening. As they engaged in discussion, the serpent seems to have had manœuvred her (or tricked her by his words into her leading him, and apparently Adam too, verse 11) to stand where the forbidden fruit was within both sight and grasp.

What does Paul have to say about this enemy?

i. *He possesses supernatural power.* Christians *do not wrestle against flesh and blood.* We are not engaged in 'conflict management' here. This is a personal contest to the death against the one who has brought down a third of the stars of heaven with a sweep of his tail (*Rev.* 12:4), and has wounded such children of God as Adam, Noah, Moses, David, Peter, and a vast multitude of others. How foolish I would be to think that I alone am exempt from his attacks or immune to his powers! His plan is to sift us like wheat, and to devour us (*Luke* 22:31; *1 Pet.* 5:8). And in addition, he is capable of transforming himself into an angel of light (*2 Cor.* 11:14).

What do we need to be able to do to overcome him? There is, ultimately, only one way *to stand* and to win: 'They have conquered him by the blood of the Lamb and by the word of their testimony, for they loved not their lives even unto death' (*Rev.* 12:11). Unreserved faithfulness to Christ is a prerequisite for enlisted soldiers in the King's army, the church militant.

This is further stressed by Paul in the way in which he notes that

ii. *He employs an organised strategy*. Paul speaks about his *schemes* (verse 11), his expert methods, his craftiness, and duplicity. (He will tell us a hundred true things, wrote the Puritan William Bridge, in order to get us to listen to the one hundred and first thing he says – the lie by which he traps us).

It would be a mistake to analyse too closely the terms Paul uses: *rulers, authorities, powers, forces*. These terms suggests that Satan's powers are well and strategically organised. Moreover his strategy is sinister (*this present darkness*), wide ranging (*cosmic*) and *spiritual*. His methods range from confrontation to deceit, ambush to conflagration, accusation to intimidation.

The Devil is called *Apollyon* (*Rev.* 9:11). As is his name, so is his nature: he is the Destroyer who seeks to destroy. Since he hates God, he hates those who love God and hates their enjoyment of God. In his cross-hairs he is always focusing on the destruction of these five things: (i) The Word of God and its reliability; (ii) The character of God and his generosity; (iii) The righteousness of God and his absolute dependability; (iv) The enjoyment of God and its abundant pleasures; (v) The fellowship of the people of God and its harmony and unity.

Be on your guard, therefore, Paul is saying. Satan is a deceiver, he is an accuser, he is a destroyer, he is a liar, and he is a blackmailer. *Be strong in the Lord and in the strength of his might* (6:10).

Is this the reason Paul's questions at the climax of Romans 8, in which he challenges all the powers that might overwhelm the Christian, all begin with 'Who' rather than 'What'?

Who [not, What] can be against us?
Who [not, What] can bring any charge against us?
Who [not, What] can condemn us?
Who [not, What] can separate us from the love of Christ?

The answer to the question 'Can Satan . . . ?' is, 'for those in Christ' No! We are 'more than conquerors through him who loved us' (*Rom.* 8:37).

In Christ alone we stand – even in, indeed *especially* in, the evil day.

36

The Armour of God

Therefore take up the whole armour of God, that you may be able to withstand in the evil day, and having done all, to stand firm. [14]*Stand therefore, having fastened on the belt of truth, and having put on the breastplate of righteousness,* [15]*and, as shoes for your feet, having put on the readiness given by the gospel of peace.* [16]*In all circumstances take up the shield of faith, with which you can extinguish all the flaming darts of the evil one;* [17]*and take the helmet of salvation, and the sword of the Spirit, which is the word of God.* (Eph. 6:13–17)

Three issues are common to battles of every kind: What is the context and nature of the battle? Who is the enemy and what is his strength? What are our resources for defence and victory?

We have seen that the watchword for spiritual warfare is 'Know your enemy'. But if we are to be victorious, we also need to know our resources and how to use them. That is certainly true of the spiritual warfare described here by Paul. Since our conflict is 'not . . . against flesh and blood' (verse 12) resources of a material kind would be hopeless against our enemy. How then can we be 'strong in the Lord and in the strength of his might' (verse 10)?

Paul's answer is by wearing *the armour of God* (verse 13).

RELIABLE ARMOUR

We ought not to think, as is sometimes suggested, that this word-picture is inspired entirely or even largely by Paul's prison experience. Paul was not the kind of prisoner who needed to be guarded by a soldier in full combat gear!

While there are clear echoes of the armour of a Roman soldier, the basic elements of 'the armour of God' are drawn from the Old Testament description of the Lord as the Divine Warrior, who is 'mighty in battle' (*Psa.* 24:8).

> But with righteousness he shall judge the poor,
> and decide with equity for the meek of the earth;
> and he shall strike the earth with the rod of his mouth,
> and with the breath of his lips he shall kill the wicked.
> Righteousness shall be the belt of his waist,
> and faithfulness the belt of his loins.
>
> (*Isa.*11:4–5)

> He saw that there was no man,
> and wondered that there was no one to intercede;
> then his own arm brought him salvation,
> and his righteousness upheld him.
> He put on righteousness as a breastplate,
> and a helmet of salvation on his head;
> he put on garments of vengeance for clothing,
> and wrapped himself in zeal as a cloak.
>
> (*Isa.* 59:16–17)

These words find their real fulfilment in our Lord Jesus Christ. He is the one who has proved the reliability of God-forged armour in the conflict against Satan.

Throughout Jesus' life, but especially in the wilderness temptations and in his passion, the armour was tested to the limit (in every respect he has been tempted as we are, yet without sin, *Heb.* 4:15). He came into the world to destroy the works of the devil (*1 John.* 3:8). Engaging in hand to hand conflict with him and experiencing the full force of his stratagems, the Lord Jesus has demonstrated that when properly worn the armour God provides will protect the one who wears it.

UNITED WE STAND

Throughout Ephesians, Paul's verbs are frequently in the second person ('you'). To be more precise they appear in the second person *plural* ('you all').

This does not imply that Paul's teaching lacks individual, personal reference to each member of the church. It is essential that we take things to heart for ourselves. But we ought not to *limit* what he says to individual activity.

This is especially true when it comes to spiritual conflict. Then it is particularly important for us to 'maintain the unity of the Spirit' (4:3), since Satan's strategy is often to 'divide and conquer'. He finds gaps in the armour and easily pierces them. A favourite tactic, as Peter knew to his pain and warned us about, is the way he seeks 'someone to devour' (*1 Pet.* 5:8). One member of the family can spoil an occasion for the whole family by demanding his or her own way, insisting on being first, or refusing to enjoy a common activity. Satan knows that if he can stir up selfishness, jealousy, or pride in just one person he can paralyse – and perhaps even destroy – a whole fellowship.

This may be one reason Paul refers to the army of God being defended by *the shield of faith*. Several different shields were available to a Roman soldier. The word used here refers to the virtually door-sized shields (they were four feet by two-and-a-half feet in size!), which were carried into battle. A tight-knit military formation behind raised shields turned a legion into a well-nigh impregnable phalanx – a solid wall of defence against the enemy.

Christians are here summoned to a similar unified mutual defence, lest the whole work of God be jeopardized by one individual being exposed and falling to the wiles of the devil!

PUTTING ON THE WHOLE ARMOUR

We are not to be 'outwitted by Satan'. We are 'not ignorant of his designs' (*2 Cor.* 2:11). Paul therefore gives us a summary guide to the armour in which we can resist the specific strategies of Satan in his relentless onslaught on believers. He specifies six pieces of armour. Each piece is important.

It would be unwise to be narrowly specific about what Paul intends us to understand by each piece of armour. But the main lines of what he says are clear.

The belt of truth must be fastened on (verse 14). This may refer to the belt that was worn in order to hold under-garments in place and to give some protection to potentially exposed parts of the body. Isaiah referred to the Divine Warrior wearing a belt of righteousness and truth ('faithfulness', *Isa.* 11:5). In view here is probably the integrity and consistency that is produced in Christians by the truth of the gospel.

God looks for 'truth', integrity and reality in the inner man (cf. *Psa.* 51:6). Earlier Paul had spoken about the evidence of this in our relationships in the church (4:25). Without this we are open to the blackmail of Satan, and over-exposed to his ability to accuse us of hypocrisy.

The breastplate of righteousness must be worn at all times (verse 14). The breastplate covered the soldier's vital organs, particularly his heart and lungs, and protected him from fatal wounding. Paul sees an analogy in this to *righteousness.*

It is difficult to be certain whether he means by this *righteousness* which is ours or righteousness which is Christ's. Perhaps, as in the case of *truth*, the two belong together in an integrated whole. The righteousness that Christ provides guards us against Satan's accusations. We sing:

> 'I may my fierce accuser face,
> And tell him Thou hast died'.[1]

We are now the recipients of an irrevocable justification (or righteousness) in Christ, which in turn leads to a growth in righteousness in ourselves.

As shoes for your feet . . . put on the readiness given by the gospel of peace (verse 15). We need to have a secure foothold. Paul's language implies that the soldier's footwear must be a help to the service of the gospel, not a hindrance to it. He must be able to keep his feet. He may be called upon to move quickly. Thus a secure grounding in the gospel enables us to be 'always . . . prepared to make a defence to anyone who asks . . . for a reason for the hope . . . ' (*1 Pet.* 3:15), always 'ready in season and out of season' to communicate the message of the gospel (*2 Tim.* 4:2). The more securely we grip

[1] From the hymn 'Approach, my soul, the mercy seat' by John Newton.

and understand the gospel of peace, the more enthusiastic we will be in communicating it (cf. *2 Cor.* 5:14–21).

The shield of faith is designed to *extinguish all the flaming darts of the evil one* (verse 16). This door-like *shield* was covered with leather. If showers of arrows, dipped in pitch and lighted, were fired towards them, the soldiers together raised their shields to form a solid wall of defence and so protect their lives.

Paul here puts his finger on a sinister and often profoundly distressing experience, well catalogued in the history of the church: a sudden, unexpected, attack on the mind, thoughts, and affections of the believer, weakening him, creating shame, spiritual paralysis and terror.

Some of the spiritual masters (like Bunyan and Spurgeon) have described experiencing an onslaught of unworthy, even blasphemous thoughts coming to them unbidden, hated as well as feared. At other times, the sudden memory of past sin seems to be like a match thrown on dry tinder. Panic and guilt overwhelm the believer; he loses his footing, doubts his salvation, and is overtaken by doubts that obscure the love of the Father.

What is the believer to do? Raise *the shield of faith*. Refuse the insidious lies that have burst into flames in the mind. Resolutely trust in Christ. Insist on the gospel – nothing in us saves us; only what Christ has done outside of us saves us. Trust in him. Christ alone is our salvation!

This is also the time to turn to others in the army and say, 'Raise your *shield of faith* over me! Pray for me and share in protecting me! Reassure me of the truth and power of the gospel!'

The helmet of salvation (verse 17) then provides essential protection. Soldiers wore the *helmet* to protect against head wounds, which again could so easily be fatal. Here, we may assume that Paul is thinking of the importance of the mind in the Christian life.

In 1 Thessalonians Paul had described the helmet as 'the hope of salvation' (*1 Thess.* 5:8). We need to learn to focus on specific truths of the gospel that will sustain us in times of intense spiritual pressure – as for example Simon Peter was enabled to do. Overcome by the shame and guilt of having betrayed his Master (he 'broke down and wept' *Mark.* 14:72), the Crumbling Rock was held in faith by the knowledge that his Lord had prayed for him that his faith would not fail (*Luke* 22:32). He wore the *helmet* – the hope of *salvation*.

The Christian who would stand against Satan must develop a mind that is well furnished with the promises of God's Word, which is able to 'make wise for salvation through faith in Christ Jesus' (*2 Tim.* 3:15).

The sword of the Spirit (verse 17) is, says Paul, *the Word of God*. As has often been recognized, this is the only weapon of attack listed as part of the armour. There are times when the best form of defence is attack. We must not only protect ourselves against the enemy; we must overcome him.

Our Lord exemplified this in the wilderness temptations, refusing Satan's blandishments but also going on the offensive by his use of God's Word and especially by his unreserved submission to it. The Christian becomes wiser than his or her enemies (*Psa. 119:98*).

If we are to do this we must learn – as we do in Psalm 119:11 – to 'store up' God's Word in our hearts, get to know it thoroughly (think of the – to us – relatively obscure verses of Scripture our Lord used against Satan!), reflecting on the different ways it can and must be applied to our lives.

If only Adam and Eve had done this in Eden!

For obvious reasons, then, Paul urges us to *put on the whole armour of God* (verse 11). Leave nothing to 'chance', no aspect of your life exposed and vulnerable. What does he mean? Simply this – to be strong in the Lord we need to take the whole Christ – Jesus Christ, Saviour and Lord, Friend and Master, Sovereign and Companion – and do so without reservation. Part armour will not adequately protect us; a part Christ will neither save nor keep us.

But what if I have already been defeated?

The fact that you recognize it is itself an encouragement; it means that there is still life and hope. The loss of a battle is not the end of the war. By God's grace you can fight again. So:

Begin to recuperate in the strength of Christ.
Consciously put on the armour.
Learn to stand and you will learn to keep standing.

37

All Prayer

Praying at all times in the Spirit, with all prayer and supplication. To that end keep alert with all perseverance, making supplication for all the saints, [19]*and also for me, that words may be given to me in opening my mouth boldly to proclaim the mystery of the gospel,* [20]*for which I am an ambassador in chains, that I may declare it boldly, as I ought to speak.* (Eph. 6:18–20)

Paul now brings his teaching on the Christian's spiritual battles to a conclusion. But his words also form the climax to the practical instruction that began in chapter four.

The section opened with an appeal based on the fact that Paul was not only an apostle but had proved his commitment to the gospel: he was a prisoner of Christ for the sake of the Gentiles (4:1). Now he closes the section by underlining his 'right' to address them: he is *an ambassador* [of Christ] *in chains*' (verse 20). Yet, at the same time, he asks them to remember him in prayer. Indeed, he calls them to *all prayer*.

Prayer itself is not seen here as part of the armour of God, but it describes the manner in which the armour is to be put on and worn. It is the atmosphere in which we are to live the Christian life, its all-embracing constant characteristic:

> 'To put your armour on,
> attend with constant prayer'.[1]

[1] From the hymn 'Soldiers of Christ arise' by Charles Wesley.

In Paul's letters the wonder and power of the gospel are so great that sometimes he must stretch human grammar and vocabulary to describe it. At other times he expresses the effects of the gospel by the way he runs words together. That is the case here. Prayer is to be made (a) *at all times* (b) *with all prayer and supplication*. In order to do that, we need to be watchful and awake, praying (c) *with all perseverance* (d) *for all the saints* (verse 18).

This is perhaps Scripture's most comprehensive single sentence on how we are to pray. Since it is also clearly an expression of Paul's own prayer disciplines, it helps us to understand how the 'God-breathed' Scriptures of Ephesians 1:15–23 and 3:14–21 are also fully and genuinely Paul's own words and indicative of the depth of his own life of prayer. What lessons on prayer does he teach us here?

SOME LESSONS ON PRAYER

We are to pray *at all times*. Prayer is not merely the action of a moment. It is a lifestyle, the focussing of a person-to-person relationship with God. It is the expression of a life lived out in the presence of God, before the face of God, in which our constant communion with God comes to conscious expression.

Prayer, then, is set within a life marked by (i) companionship and (ii) dialogue with the Lord. It is the overflow of how we live as Calvin says, *coram deo* (in the presence of God). The wise Christian therefore adopts what we might call 'the sanctuary principle': keeping within the heart a place of devotion to the Lord – from which all else is excluded.

We are to pray *in the Spirit*. This expression does not here refer to 'speaking in tongues'. Elsewhere Paul does comment on praying 'in a tongue'. He describes that activity as one in which the spirit prays but the mind or understanding is 'unfruitful' (*1 Cor.* 14:14). But here he is urging great alertness of mind (verse 18). What, then, does it mean to pray *in the Spirit*? It implies the help of the Spirit in our weakness (cf. *Rom.* 8:26–27); relying on his power and wisdom, not on our own.

The parallel we noticed earlier between being filled with the Spirit and letting the Word of Christ dwell in us richly helps us here (*Eph.* 5:18 and *Col.* 3:16). To pray *in the Spirit* is to be filled with the Spirit as we pray. This means submitting our mind, thoughts, will, and desires to be influenced and mastered by God's Word. We thus begin 'to think God's thoughts after him', develop instincts that are aligned to his will, and ask for those things that he has revealed please him and that he promises to do.

In essence, prayer involves bringing God's promises back to him, in the context of all that he has told us about himself, his character, and his will, and saying, 'Father, you are all that you have revealed yourself to be; you will keep all the promises you have made . . . *therefore* I come to you to ask for. . .'.

To pray with *all prayer and supplication* may simply mean to offer prayers of all kinds – adoration, confession, thanksgiving, and intercession – always made in the spirit of a servant approaching his or her Master, a subject coming with his or her petitions to the Great King.

Prayer of this order is the expression of a full and a disciplined life of communion with God. Unselfconsciously Paul had earlier illustrated this in the prayers he expressed for the Ephesians.

There we saw him with knees bowed but eyes gazing upwards, far beyond the visible realms to the Lord enthroned in majesty and glory 'far above all rule and authority and power and dominion, and above every name that is named' (1:21).

In addition Paul rejoices in God's activity in the world and overflows with praise: 'I do not cease to give thanks for you'. He sees clearly what God's people need: 'remembering you in my prayers that the God of our Lord Jesus Christ, the Father of glory, may give you a spirit of wisdom and of revelation in the knowledge of him' (1:16–17; cf. 3:14–21).

The Ephesians need to *keep alert with all perseverance*. As if in a flashback to his Lord's urgent words, 'Be on your guard, keep awake' (*Mark* 13:33) and, 'Watch and pray that you may not enter into temptation' (*Mark*. 14:38), Paul urges keeping our wits about us. The verb *keep alert* has the basic meaning of staying awake – it was used of shepherds watching their sheep, their task all the more necessary because of the presence of wolves and other wild beasts that threatened the flock. Christ is building his church on territory that has been occupied by an enemy. Alertness is always essential when living in a war zone.

The New Testament has more than one word for *perseverance*. The term here implies a resolute determination to see something through to its conclusion. God hears our prayers immediately (he knows what we need before we ask). But there is almost always a time lag between our asking and our recognizing his answer. Prayer engages us in the world of spiritual warfare. We may discover, as Daniel did (cf. *Dan*. 10:1ff.), that our intercession sets off a chain of events that in turn increases spiritual hostility. Rugged stickability may well be required before it becomes clear to us that God heard our prayers the moment we expressed them.

Thus we live *making supplication for all the saints*. We pray *with* the whole church whenever we say '*Our* Father . . .' But we are also to pray *for* the church. This meant that the Ephesians should pray not only for their own assembly, but for other assemblies of the Lord; not only praying about their own burdens, but about the concerns of their fellow believers – in an ever widening circle of intercession.

In churches where this principle comes to expression seasons of prayer can become lessons in geography as well as spirituality. Those who live in small or remote spheres discover that all the earth is the Lord's and all places are equidistant from his throne. No stronghold of Satan is safe from the remotest saint who knows what it is to pray!

In addition to these general principles, Paul adds a personal prayer request.

PRAY FOR ME!

It is natural for Christians to think and speak of Paul as the 'mighty apostle', even although he thought of himself as 'the very least of all the saints' (*Eph*. 3:8). He was weak, sometimes in deeply distressing circumstances, at times lonely and afraid; he was not a stranger to despairing of life itself (*2 Cor.* 1:3–11). He needed the help of the prayers of his friends (cf. *Phil.* 1:19).

Here however he asks that prayer would be specifically focused on his proclamation of the gospel. The request is not unique (cf. *2 Thess.* 3:1ff.; *Col.* 4:3). But it is arresting. He asks the Ephesians to join him in prayer for two things he regards as essential in his ministry:

(i) First he senses a need that *words may be given* to him. Presumably Paul did not find language itself difficult, even if he did not employ the rhetorical techniques of the philosophers and orators. What he is asking for is not merely *words* as sounds, but *words* that will penetrate; not mere eloquence, or accuracy of vocabulary, but words that issued from his lips in the power of the Holy Spirit (cf. *1 Cor*. 2:4–5; *1 Thess.* 1:5).

(ii) Paul also asked the Ephesians to pray for *boldness* to characterize him. Why? Because he constantly faced persecution. Satan uses people, and in using them dehumanizes them, turning the apparently mild-mannered into vicious spiritual thugs. Intimidation is one of his favoured tactics. Paul needed courage to stand against it.

But he needed similar *boldness* when ministering God's Word inside the church. For when the preaching of the Word begins to break into human hearts, it exposes in some a sinful desire for power and position within the church. It gets under their skin, inside their consciences, and reveals their failures, pride, self-centredness, and their driving desire for influence or their own reputation. It unmasks hypocrisy.

There are few more dangerous things in the life of a Christian fellowship than those who are enraged when the truth about them is exposed by the Word of God. They may well attack the messenger and, failing to destroy him, will seek to destroy the entire fellowship rather than repent. Several of Paul's letters indicate that he was no stranger to such viciousness.

Did people ever tell Paul to 'go easy', to shape his ministry to the tastes of his hearers, not to ruffle influential feathers, not to risk losing some and thus endanger his influence, or more subtly, diminish his reputation? But Paul was a spiritual physician, a skilled surgeon of the S(s)pirit. The Word cuts in order to heal. If it is the sword of the Spirit against Satan, it is also the scalpel of the Lord for the physician of souls to use in preaching.

Whoever would speak boldly like this for Christ needs prayer. Hence Paul's appeal.

Ministers of the gospel today need much prayer if their congregations are to hear preaching that expresses this apostolic boldness. Make sure you pray for them.

If you are a minister, know that no one needs more prayer than you do. Make sure you ask for it. Do not pretend that you labour in your own strength. Remember C. H. Spurgeon's reply to the question, 'What is the secret of your ministry?': 'My people pray for me.'

38

Final Greetings

So that you also may know how I am and what I am doing, Tychicus the beloved brother and faithful minister in the Lord will tell you everything. [22]*I have sent him to you for this very purpose, that you may know how we are, and that he may encourage your hearts.*

[23]*Peace be to the brothers, and love with faith, from God the Father and the Lord Jesus Christ.* [24]*Grace be with all who love our Lord Jesus Christ with love incorruptible.* (Eph. 6:21–24)

Why did Paul write the letter to the Ephesians? He wanted his friends to *know how I am and what I am doing*. The reason for the letter may be as simple (and sweet) as that. He had many friends whom he had not seen for some time. He was now in prison and, given the way news could be readily exchanged in the Roman Empire, his friends may well have heard and become over-anxious about him.

Perhaps Paul remembered how worried he himself had once been about his friend Titus. On that occasion he wrote: 'When I came to Troas to preach the gospel of Christ, even though a door was opened for me in the Lord, my spirit was not at rest because I did not find my brother Titus there. So I took leave of them and went on to Macedonia' (*2 Cor.* 2:12–13). Knowing such distress was in part a preparation for ministry to the distressed, as he recognized on more than one occasion (*2 Cor.* 1:3–11; cf. *Phil.* 1: 12–14).

So he was sending *Tychicus the beloved brother and faithful minister* to *tell* his friends *everything* (verse 21).

TYCHICUS

Tychicus is one of the unsung heroes of the New Testament church.

Why did Paul send him? The few references we find to Tychicus in the New Testament show him to have been a man of considerable spiritual stature. He was originally from Asia (*Acts* 20:4), possibly from Ephesus itself. He joined Paul's apostolic band and served as a trusted colleague. He carried this letter and the letter to the Colossians (and also the 'letter from Laodicaea', *Col.* 4:16 – if it was a different letter from this one – to the Ephesians).

Tychicus was also accompanying Onesimus, the once-runaway-now-converted slave back to Colossae (cf. the Letter to Philemon, which Tychicus also presumably carried). It says a great deal about his Christian character, grace, and wisdom that he was entrusted with 'brokering' the return of a slave to his Christian master as well as carrying the apostle's precious teaching. At the end of Paul's life, he stood with him in his days of imprisonment until, anxious to see his dear Timothy, Paul sent him again to Ephesus in the hope that Timothy would be able to come to see him one last time (2 *Tim.* 4:12 – did Tychicus also carry 2 Timothy?).

It is very possible, then, that Tychicus had also acted as Paul's scribe, perhaps even discussing with Paul the contents of Ephesians! He may well have been the first minister to expound Ephesians to a congregation!

Here, then, in what seems to be a passing reference of no real significance, we find a pattern that regularly appears in Paul's letters: the individuals he mentions are living illustrations, working models of the truth he is expounding and the lifestyle to which we are called by the gospel.

Tychicus adds Paul, can be trusted to *tell you everything*. Does this mean more than 'everything about me, Paul'? Does it also mean, 'If you need something in this letter explained, if you wonder how this works out in the life of your fellowship, or in your home and family, or if you are struggling to put this teaching on holiness into practice, or are still puzzled by the teaching on election – ask Tychicus . . . he will *tell you everything*.'

In addition, Tychicus was sent by Paul *that he may encourage your hearts* (verse 22). Together these two men went out of their way to be the hands of the Holy Spirit (the Heavenly Paraclete-Encourager). They saw that as a chief function of their ministry.

This should, surely, lead us to pause to pray, 'Lord, in my generation, in my sphere of service, in my fellowship, please make me like Tychicus.'

Paul was prepared to send out the best men he knew to help others, and did not keep them jealously for himself. There is a lesson here for the whole church.

THE BENEDICTION

Ephesians began with a Doxology – a word (*logos*) of praise to the glory (*doxa*) of God. It now concludes with a Benediction – a pronouncement of blessing from God. The Doxology blessed God – spoke well of him – for his blessing – speaking well of – us in Christ. Now Paul closes his letter by speaking well of the Ephesians (and all believing readers of this letter) in the name of the Lord.

In the introduction Paul praised the Father for what he has done for us and given to us through his Son, all of which is brought to us by the Spirit. Now in the conclusion he traces the blessings brought to us by the Spirit back to their source in the Son and the Father, and thus brings a gracious closure to all that he has taught us.

Just as Tychicus can be seen as embodying the lifestyle which the whole letter had endorsed, the benediction perfectly summarises the blessings in Christ that the whole letter has expounded. Thus Paul gives what amounts to a threefold summary of the blessings we receive and the hallmark of the life to which it leads. The Letter began with grace and peace to all who had faith. It ends with peace and love with faith for all those who have tasted grace.

Paul wishes *peace . . . to the brothers*. This is not only the cessation of hostilities, but the re-establishing in working order of broken relationships. It is *shalom*, well-being. It comes from being set free from the dark powers that bind and destroy us, from being reconciled to God in Christ, and subsequently working this out in relationship to others. Paul has given us rich and penetrating teaching on how that has been accomplished, and what *shalom* looks like in the most basic relationships of life (chapters 5–6).

In addition, Paul prays that his readers will experience *love with faith from God the Father and the Lord Jesus Christ.* God has demonstrated his love for us in his election, in the work of Christ, and in the presence of his Spirit in our lives. Paul has expounded how that love is expressed in us and through us (chapters 3–5). He has also explained that faith does not come naturally to us, for we are spiritually dead and insensitive to God by nature. But he has brought us to faith, raising us from spiritual death, delivering us from spiritual bondage, and adopting us into his family (chapters 1–2).

The letter closes with a prayer for the blessing of the whole church of God. *Grace be with all who love our Lord Jesus Christ with love incorruptible.* Here, then, at the end, we return to the beginning, to the source of all blessing and the cause of all doxology: grace, God's love and favour displayed in Jesus Christ to sinners. Without grace we are spiritually dead, blind, lost, enslaved, guilty, and condemned.

Paul had already prayed that his readers' spiritual sight would be illumined to see and grasp the immensity of this divine love (*Eph.* 3:17b–21). When that love is received it is met with an answering love – a love that cannot be corrupted, a love that will never die, a love that will last for all eternity.

The apostle's closing desire, then, is that the grace he has expounded will be the grace that we have experienced. If so, our love for the Lord will be a love that is undying.

That is what Ephesians was written to teach us.

Blessed be the God and Father of our Lord Jesus Christ,
who has blessed us in Christ
with every spiritual blessing
in the heavenly places!

Group Study Guide

SCHEME FOR GROUP BIBLE STUDY
(Covers 13 Weeks; before each study read the passage indicated and the chapters from this book shown below.)

	Study Passage	Chapters
1.	Ephesians 1:1–2	Introduction and ch. 1
2.	Ephesians 1:3–14	2–4
3.	Ephesians 1:15–23	5–7
4.	Ephesians 2:1–10	8–11
5.	Ephesians 2:11–22	12–15
6.	Ephesians 3:1–13	16–18
7.	Ephesians 3:14–21	19–20
8.	Ephesians 4:1–16	21–23
9.	Ephesians 4:17–32	24–25
10.	Ephesians 5:1–21	26–29
11.	Ephesians 5:22–33	30–31
12.	Ephesians 6:1–9	32–34
13.	Ephesians 6:10–24	35–38

This Study Guide has been prepared for group Bible study, but it can also be used individually. Those who use it on their own may find it helpful to keep a note of their responses in a notebook.

The way in which group Bible studies are led can greatly enhance their value. A well-conducted study will appear as though it has been easy to lead, but that is usually because the leader has worked hard and planned well. Clear aims are essential.

AIMS

In all Bible study, individual or corporate, we have several aims:

1. To gain an understanding of the original meaning of the particular passage of Scripture;
2. To apply this to ourselves and our own situation;
3. To develop some specific ways of putting the biblical teaching into practice.

2 Timothy 3:16–17 provides a helpful structure. Paul says that Scripture is useful for:

(i) teaching us;
(ii) rebuking us;
(iii) correcting, or changing us;
(iv) training us in righteousness.

Consequently, in studying any passage of Scripture, we should always have in mind these questions:

What does this passage teach us (about God, ourselves, etc.)?

Does it rebuke us in some way?

How can its teaching transform us?

What equipment does it give us for serving Christ?

In fact, these four questions alone would provide a safe guide in any Bible study.

PRINCIPLES

In group Bible study we meet in order to learn about God's Word and ways 'with all the saints' (*Eph.* 3:18). But our own experience, as well as Scripture, tells us that the saints are not always what they *are* called to be in every situation – including group Bible study! Leaders ordinarily have to work hard and prepare well if the work of the group is to be spiritually profitable. The following guidelines for leaders may help to make this a reality.

Preparation:

1. Study and understand the passage yourself. The better prepared and more sure of the direction of the study you are, the more likely

it is that the group will have a beneficial and enjoyable study. Ask: What are the main things this passage is saying? How can this be made clear? This is not the same question as the more common 'What does this passage "say to you"?', which expects a reaction rather than an exposition of the passage. Be clear about that dis-tinction yourself, and work at making it clear in the group study.

2. On the basis of your own study form a clear idea *before* the group meets of (i) the main theme(s) of the passage which should be opened out for discussion, and (ii) some general conclusions the group ought to reach as a result of the study. Here the questions which arise from 2 Timothy 3:16–17 should act as our guide.

3. The guidelines and questions which follow may help to provide a general framework for each discussion; leaders should use them as starting places which can be further developed. It is usually help-ful to have a specific goal or theme in mind for group discussion, and one is suggested for each study. But even more important than tracing a single theme is understanding the teaching and the implications of the passage.

Leading the Group:

1. Announce the passage and theme for the study, and begin with prayer. In group studies it may be helpful to invite a different person to lead in prayer each time you meet.

2. Introduce the passage and theme, briefly reminding people of its outline and highlighting the content of each subsidiary section.

3. Lead the group through the discussion questions. Use your own if you are comfortable in doing so; those provided may be used, developing them with your own points. As discussion proceeds, continue to encourage the group first of all to discuss the significance of the passage (teaching) and only then its application (meaning for us). It may be helpful to write important points and applications on a board by way of summary as well as visual aid.

4. At the end of each meeting, remind members of the group of their assignments for the next meeting, and encourage them to come prepared. Be sufficiently prepared as the leader to give specific assignments to individuals, or even couples or groups, to come with specific contributions.

5. Remember that you are the leader of the group! Encourage clear contributions, and do not be embarrassed to ask someone to explain what they have said more fully or to help them to do so ('Do you mean . . . ?').

Most groups include the 'over-talkative', the 'over-silent' and the 'red-herring raisers'! Leaders must control the first, encourage the second and redirect the third! Each leader will develop his or her own most natural way of doing that; but it will be helpful to think out what that is before the occasion arises! The first two groups can be helped by some judicious direction of questions to specific individuals or even groups (for example, 'Jane, you know something about this from personal experience . . .'); the third by redirecting the discussion to the passage itself ('That is an interesting point, but isn't it true that this passage really concentrates on . . . ?'). It may be helpful to break the group up into smaller groups sometimes, giving each subgroup specific points to discuss and to report back on. A wise arranging of these smaller groups may also help each member to participate.

More important than any techniques we may develop is the help of the Spirit enabling us to understand and to apply the Scriptures. Have and encourage a humble, prayerful spirit.

6. Keep faith with the schedule; it is better that some of the group wished the study could have been longer than that others are inconvenienced by it stretching beyond the time limits set.

7. Close in prayer. As time permits, spend the closing minutes in corporate prayer, encouraging the group to apply what they have learned in praise and thanks, intercession and petition.

STUDY 1

Introduction and Chapter 1

AIM: To study the context of Paul's Letter to the Ephesians and to apply some of the lessons found in its opening words.

1. What do we learn about Paul from the various ways in which he describes himself and his care for the Ephesians in this letter? (See especially: 1:1; 1:15–16; 2:3–5,10; 3:1; 3: 7–8, 13; 4:1; 6:18–20, 22.)
2. In an age of telephone calls and cyberspace what value is there in Christians continuing to write letters?
3. The church is often described as 'One, Holy, Catholic and Apostolic'. What do you understand these terms to mean, and how biblical are they?
4. What difference does it make to your Christian life to understand that you are a 'saint'?
5. 'The gospel . . . has a grammar' (Ferguson, p. 4). What does this mean?

STUDY 2

Chapters 2–4

AIM: To learn to appreciate the blessings which have come to us in Jesus Christ.

1. How do we receive and experience every spiritual blessing in Christ?
2. If Paul's teaching on election causes controversy, what are the important things to remember when we talk about it?
3. How would you explain to someone else what Paul meant by 'mystery'?
4. What are the three major features of our fallen world with which Christ came to deal? How important is this for our understanding and communicating the gospel?
5. 'All suspicion of niggardliness on the part of God dissolves . . . ' (Ferguson, p. 15). What does this mean? Why is it important?
6. What is the Christian's inheritance? What other passages of Scripture shed light on it?

7. How is the knowledge of God's sovereignty 'medicine' (Ferguson, pp. 17–18)?

8. Is knowing God as Trinity important for practical Christian living.

STUDY 3

Chapters 5–7

AIM: To study Paul's prayer, and to learn from it how to focus prayer and to grow in prayer.

1. Ferguson speaks about 'the resulting fruit in our lives of God's electing grace'. What is this fruit, how is it produced, and how important is it to the Christian life?

2. What do you think are the most obvious contrasts or similarities between the way Paul prayed and the way we pray? What can we learn about this for individual and corporate prayer?

3. Paul prays for three particular things for the Ephesians. How can we pray these same things for our fellow Christians?

4. How would you use this passage to encourage a church or an individual Christian who was paralysed by fears?

5. In what other passages does Paul speak about the church as the body of Christ? What are the recurring themes in his teaching on this subject?

STUDY 4

Chapters 8–11

AIM: To understand the nature and effects of sin, and in the light of this to learn to appreciate the power and wonder of the gospel and the way it transforms life.

1. In what ways do you think people today are deceived about their true spiritual condition? How do you think Scripture teaches us to help them?

2. How does Paul describe Satan and his activity here? What other passages in the New Testament shed further light on his work?

3. What are the evidences that people are 'by nature children of wrath'? Why does Ferguson say that to be 'in the flesh' is to be in 'a world order, an all-encompassing reality'?

4. Why does Paul 'linger long and lovingly on the thought of God's goodness' (p. 48)? Why is it important not to 'fall into the error of thinking that the love, grace and kindness of God are the result of the work of Christ' (p. 48)?

5. Use Ephesians 2:8–10 to explain what it means to become a Christian.

STUDY 5

Chapters 12–15

AIM: To study Paul's teaching on God's saving grace to the Gentile world and the implications of Jew and Gentile believers being one in Christ.

1. Why is it important for a Christian to 'remember' his or her past? Should we not forget it? Is Paul contradicting what he says in Philippians 3:13?

2. Would it make any difference to your life if you wrote your own obituary notice today?

3. What is the 'big picture' (Ferguson, chapter 13) and how important is it?

4. 'Christ preaches' – how important is this for our learning how to listen to preaching?

5. In what ways should the church today be 'built on the apostles'?

STUDY 6

Chapters 16–18

AIM: To consider the special role to which God called Saul of Tarsus, and to reflect on how God's grace and wisdom are seen in the gospel and the church.

1. Should every Christian have a sense that their lives are for others in specific ways?

2. Is it surprising that anyone today should be reading a two-thousand-year-old letter written by an apostle?

3. Should all Christians be able to describe themselves as 'the very least of all the saints', or is that unique to Paul?
4. In what ways do you think God might be displaying his wisdom (a) in your church fellowship and (b) in your own life?
5. How can our sufferings be for the glory of others?

STUDY 7

Chapters 19–20

AIM: To deepen appreciation for prayer, and to gain a better sense of the wonder of the love of Christ for us and his dwelling in us.

1. What chiefly impresses you about Paul's prayer in 3:14–19?
2. How does the New Testament describe, explain, and expound the indwelling of Christ?
3. What does it mean to 'know' the love of Christ? How can we get to know it better?
4. In what ways should we be encouraged by God's ability and power?
5. How do you think the glory of God should be seen in your church fellowship?

STUDY 8

Chapters 21–23

AIM: To consider Paul's teaching on the church, its unity, diversity, ministry, and growth.

1. How important is humility and what are the hallmarks of its presence in a Christian?
2. What particular things challenge your patience? How might Paul's teaching help you to grow in patience?
3. How does this passage help us to think more clearly about the use of spiritual gifts in the church?
4. Paul had pastored the church in Ephesus and left them a model for ministry. Consult Acts 20:17–38. What stands out in his ministry? In what ways is this a model for ministry today?

5. How does the ministry of the Word accomplish what Paul says here (a) in your own life and (b) in your church fellowship?
6. How important is integrity?

STUDY 9

Chapters 24–25

AIM: To study in detail how and why Christians are different from non Christians.

1. In what ways do you see Paul's description of unbelievers replicated in people today?
2. Why is it so important that we realize the new identity that God has given us in Christ?
3. How do we 'put away' the old?
4. What is the 'replacement principle' in sanctification and why is it important?
5. Read over the specific areas of necessary transformation described by Paul. In each case, consider how it can take place.

STUDY 10

Chapters 26–29

AIM: To focus on the ways in which being a Christian leads to living a life marked by love, light, and wisdom.

1. What is love, and how can we be commanded to exercise it?
2. What motivation does Paul give us in this passage, and how does it work?
3. How important is thanksgiving in the Christian life? What does Paul contrast it with, and why?
4. How would you help someone who asked you how they should go about discovering God's will for their life?
5. What does wisdom look like in practice?
6. How do we obey the command to 'be filled with the Spirit' and what are the evidences that we are?

STUDY 11

Chapters 30–31

AIM: To learn the Bible's teaching about marriage and to work its implications in practical ways.

1. How is the health of marriage 'essential both to the church and to society in general'? What influences do you see undermining this, and how can they be resisted?
2. What do you consider to be the most important elements of a wife's attitude to and relationship with her husband?
3. What are the hallmarks of a husband's love for his wife? What would they look like in practical terms in your life?
4. In what ways do you think Satan might attack Christian marriages today, and why?
5. How should a husband and wife deal with differences of opinion? Should they ever have them?

STUDY 12

Chapters 32–34

AIM: To study Paul's teaching on relationships in the family and in the workplace and to apply them to situations today.

1. Why are parents afraid to teach their children to obey?
2. Does Paul's use of one of the Ten Commandments really say anything about his understanding of how the other Commandments should be used by Christians?
3. In what ways do you think fathers today might provoke their children to anger? How can this be avoided?
4. What practical counsel would you give to a prospective father to get himself ready to bring up his children in the nurture of the Lord?
5. How would you apply Paul's teaching on masters and slaves to the society in which you live today?

STUDY 13

Chapters 35–38

AIM: To learn the nature of the spiritual warfare in which we are engaged and to apply Paul's teaching on the way the armour of God is to be worn.

1. While Paul does not specify what the schemes of Satan are, what do you think he might have had in mind?
2. What warning signals should Genesis 3 send to us?
3. How did Jesus use the armour of God?
4. How do we put on the various pieces of armour, which Paul describes?
5. What special wiles of the devil do we need to be on our guard against today?
6. Does Paul's willingness to send some of his best friends and most trusted colleagues to help other churches have anything to teach us in the church today?
7. Looking back over your study of Ephesians, what are the most important lessons you feel you have learned?

FOR FURTHER READING

The following commentaries are more detailed than the exposition in this volume, but can be read without special technical skills that are demanded by many recent commentaries.

JOHN CALVIN, *The Epistles of Paul the Apostle to the Galatians, Ephesians, Philippians and Colossians*, translated by T. H. L. Parker, edited by D. W. and T. F. Torrance; Edinburgh: Oliver and Boyd, 1965.

WILLIAM HENDRIKSEN, *Ephesians*, in *Galatians and Ephesians*, Edinburgh: Banner of Truth, 1972.

CHARLES HODGE, *A Commentary on the Epistle to the Ephesians* London: Banner of Truth, 1964.